Your Resume:
Key to a Better Job

Leonard Corwen

Macmillan • USA

Sixth Edition

Macmillan General Reference
A Simon & Schuster Macmillan Company
1633 Broadway
New York, NY 10019-6783

An Arco Book

Arco, Prentice Hall, and colophons are
registered trademarks of Simon & Schuster, Inc.

Library of Congress Cataloging-in-Publication Data

ISBN 0-02-860343-5

Manufactured in the United States of America

2   3   4   5   6   7   8   9   10

CONTENTS

Part Two
Getting The Job

INDEX OF RESUMES
BY JOB TITLE

Foreword

When firms were smaller and the business of hiring less complicated, a job interview could usually be gotten by knocking on an office door. An applicant and his prospective employer would meet face-to-face, with a minimum of ceremony, and if both got along, the interview would result in a job offer.

Today, if you make a cold call on a company, you will be lucky if you get past the security guard in the lobby. The best you can hope for is the privilege of filling out a six-page application form which eventually will wend its way into the personnel files, some of which, in today's large corporate structures, resemble the Library of Congress.

Gone are the days when the personnel function was delegated to office managers, assistants, and even secretaries and clerks. Companies today are highly structured with the personnel department a top management function commanding high priorities in budget and staff. Personnel managers are concerned with wage and salary administration, labor relations, union negotiations, government regulations, and a myriad of other activities, leaving little time for speculative interviews and haphazard hiring.

So, to get your foot in the door, you must put your resume in the mail. For better or worse, this letter-sized sheet of paper is, in most cases, your only key to the interview. Therefore, it is imperative for the serious job seeker to know how to prepare the right resume for himself, one which will stand out above the others and get him or her the all-important interview.

What is the *right* resume? If you speak to five different experts and read three books on the subject, you will probably come up with eight ways to concoct the right resume. Still, there are standard rules for good resume writing which, although flexible enough to meet individual requirements, should be followed for best results.

Of the hundreds of resumes which cross my desk every week, I can tell which will result in an immediate interview and which will be passed over. Unfortunately, those which will evoke interest in the reader constitute only a small percentage of the total. There are many reasons for this, most having to do with the resume itself and some with the accompanying letters and material.

The point is, there is a wrong way and a right way to write a resume and in such a vital activity as your career you must give yourself every advantage.

In Part One of this book, you will be taken step-by-step through the preparation and writing of a resume and cover letter designed especially for you. A Personal Assessment Inventory will enable you to determine what to put into your resume and, more important, what to leave out. You will see that although every resume must contain basic information, there are several forms it can take, each designed with a specific objective in mind. Each form is analyzed and samples are provided for your guidance in constructing your own resume.

However, even the best resume may not receive the attention it deserves unless it is marketed properly. This book, therefore, tells you how to merchandise your resume. The busy personnel manager who receives hundreds of resumes in reply to a classified advertisement must delegate the initial screening activity to an assistant, whose usual function is to choose those resumes which fit the job requirements. However, in practice, resumes are often given a quick screening, and instead of a hunt for qualifications that fit the job specifications, it becomes a hunt for information that will disqualify you.

This means that in order to be chosen for an interview you have to write a resume and cover letter that outline your qualifications clearly and forcefully. Otherwise they will probably find their way into the files, never to see the light of day again.

Part Two will tell you how to conduct your job search. Answering "help wanted" advertising is the most obvious method of finding job openings. If you know how to select and answer these ads properly, you can save a lot of time and effort. Advertised jobs, however, represent only a very small percentage of total available jobs.

The direct-mail approach is one of the most effective ways to locate the hidden job market which comprises about 80% to 85% of available job openings, openings which are not advertised or made public. How this is done is covered in this book, together with a directory of sources of information arranged by occupation, plus a list of general business and industrial directories.

Everyone knows that employment agencies and headhunters play a major role in matching employers with available applicants. But how to use them effectively is not as well known. The chapter on how to choose and use employment agencies will show you how to get the most out of them.

You can't get a good job without an interview—and chances are you can't get that interview without the right resume combined with a skillfull, well-programmed job-hunting plan.

This book will help you to decide what kind of job you want, how to prepare a resume that will sell your special capabilities, and how to effectively plan your job hunt.

The first thing you must do, after deciding what kind of job you want, is to prepare a resume that will sell *you* to a prospective employer. The competition for jobs is always keen and your resume can determine whether or not you get to the next step, the interview.

But even at a friendly interview, a competent, experienced applicant with superior qualifications can flunk by not being adequately prepared and not having the necessary information about the company. There are also certain rules of behavior that should be followed during an interview. These rules are spelled out in the chapter on interviewing, together with a description of the different types of interviews and how to handle them. A list of probable questions you may be asked is also included.

The success or failure of any worthwhile activity hinges to a great extent upon the way you use your time. Because job hunting can be a lengthy and expensive activity, it is vital that you use your available time effectively. Tips on how to do this are shown.

To help you keep track of all of the letters, telephone calls and, hopefully, interviews, several forms and control sheets have been included. The proper use of these forms will help you stay on top of your campaign.

If you are a beginner looking for your first job, you will benefit from the experience of others who have struggled their way through interviews before hitting the right formula. If you are a veteran job applicant, it will do you no harm to review some of the rules that you might have forgotten since your last job search.

Looking for a job, whether you are unemployed or working but want a better position, isn't easy. It is an unpleasant and sometimes frightening experience. But like all tasks, if it is done properly, the results will be satisfying.

In the back of this book you will find a bibliography listing the most up-to-date and useful books on resumes and related topics. They will benefit you in what can be a rewarding search for your job.

TOMORROW'S JOBS

By the year 2000, the United States will have 21 million more workers and an economy 40% larger than today's, according to projections prepared by the Bureau of Labor Statistics. An expanding economy and increased demand for goods and services will create millions of jobs in almost every type of occupation between now and the end of the century. Growth will be especially strong for technicians, professionals, service workers, administrators, managers and marketing and sales workers.

Where will the jobs be? The U.S. Department of Labor, looking for the fastest growing occupations through the end of this century, fed countless bits of information into a computer. Here is a partial list of what came out, with the projected percentage change:

Paralegals	75.3%
Medical Assistants	70.0%
Home Health Aides	67.9%
Data Processing Equipment Repairers	61.2%
Operations Research Analysts	55.4%
Physical Therapists	57.0%
Travel Agents	54.1%
Financial Services Workers	53.8%
Computer Systems Analysts	53.3%
Physical Therapy Assistants	52.5%
Occupational Therapists	48.8%
Computer Programmers	48.1%
Human Services Workers	44.9%
Nurses	38.0%
Accountants and Auditors	22.0%
Teachers, Secondary Schools	19.0%
Salespersons, Retail	19.0%

Nearly four out of five jobs will be in industries that provide services. Jobs will be found in small firms as well as in large corporations, in all levels of government and in industries as diverse as banking, advertising, media and communications, hospitals, ecology and conservation, law enforcement, data processing, and management consulting. The two largest industry groups, health services and business services, are projected to continue their rapid growth.

Because of the rapid expansion of health care employment, 7 of the 10 fastest-growing occupations will be in health-related fields. Hospitals, outpatient care facilities, offices of health care practitioners, and nursing homes will be hard-pressed to find trained, qualified people to fill the demand for services.

Business service industries are projected to employ 8.3 million workers by the year 2000. Business services also includes the fastest growing industry in the economy—computer and data processing services. This industry is expected to grow five times faster than the average for all industries, due to a rapidly increasing demand from business firms, government agencies and individuals. Research, management and consulting are also expected to have very rapid growth.

In addition to generating millions of clerical, sales and service jobs, the service sector will also create jobs for financial managers, engineers, nurses, electrical and electronics technicians and many other managerial, professional, and technical workers. The fastest-growing occupations will be those that require the most educational preparation.

One final factor to remember when measuring the outlook for an occupation is that growth of employment is only one reason for job openings. Even occupations with little or no employment growth may still offer many opportunities. In fact, most openings arise because of the need to replace workers who leave the occupation and transfer to other jobs as a step up the career ladder, or change careers. Other workers leave the job market to return to school, to assume household responsibilities, or to go into business. The continuing trend toward earlier retirement remains another major factor in creating job vacancies. As a result, even occupations with slower than average growth may offer many jobs for new workers.

Part One
Writing the Resume and
Cover Letter

Chapter 1

WHAT IS A RESUME?

While you are out job hunting, you are going to hear about resumes so often that you will probably dream about them. Since your search for a job will be so closely tied to this vital document, a discussion of what it really is and how it can affect you as a job hunter is in order.

The word "resume" is a French word that, according to Webster, means "a summing up, a summary, a condensed statement, or a short history." It is your autobiography, condensed to fit a #10 envelope—and it is no simple task to write. In fact, it would be easier to write a full-length book about yourself than to cram your adult life into a one- or two-page summary. Your resume is like a snapshot, which, once developed, becomes a permanent reflection of you. And, since it will probably precede you in all of your dealings with prospective employers, it must be the best image you can project. Otherwise, you will be among the thousands of eager, qualified job applicants who walk the streets or sit at home or at the office waiting for the mail that never comes, the phone that never rings, and the job that never materializes.

The Paper Applicant

Are resumes important? You better believe it! The competition to attract an employer's attention is keen, bitter, and brutal. You need every tool you can get, and at the outset your resume is the only one you have.

John T., a disgruntled, discouraged job seeker, an executive with many years of successful experience, sat across from my desk one afternoon. His company had just been swallowed up by a huge conglomerate whose computers, in their impersonal wisdom, decided that after ten years of service, he was surplus. He had been given the opportunity to resign, a term which modern corporations use to replace the old-fashioned "you're fired." Losing his job after long and loyal service was not his principal concern. He took that philosophically. But after a month of looking, what really upset him was the fact, as he put it, that he was turning into paper.

It seemed that there was little interest in him as a flesh-and-blood human being. Every help wanted advertisement he read asked for a resume, and wanted it mailed, generally to a box number. How, he wondered, could anyone rely on a self-serving sheet of paper to determine his personal qualifications? A chimpanzee, he said, could be taught to push a button that would automatically type any resume that had been programmed. When he visited employment agencies, executive recruiters, and personal contacts, he was met with a quick glance, generally just searching enough to determine if he was wearing trousers, and then almost without exception, asked for his resume—sometimes even before a handshake if it was proffered.

John was angry and bewildered. After years of satisfactory personal relationships, and high-level decision making in important company matters, he was beginning to feel invisible. No one seemed to be interested in him as a person. As a result he found himself reviewing and rewriting his resume constantly, trying to tailor it individually to every job he applied for. He was getting good at it too, and what was frightening him was that he was beginning to enjoy it. One day the realization hit him that he was becoming a professional resume writer, getting more

1

satisfaction out of completing a new version of his life history than anticipating the prospect of an interview and a job.

By the time he came in to see me, he was completely demoralized. "Why," he asked, "was the resume considered so important a document that it was impossible to get an interview without it?"

Necessity or Habit?

His problem was not unique, and he was not exaggerating. The practice of requiring resumes before an invitation for an interview grew after World War II, not only because job applicants suddenly descended upon the market in great numbers, but also because companies began to expand so rapidly, that it was not possible to personally interview all of the applicants who were on the market at that time. Like so many practices that begin as necessities, the resume requirement has become fixed, and in too many cases, a crutch for personnel managers who find it an easy way to screen applicants.

Even when there is plenty of time for face-to-face meetings, the habit of requiring resumes instead of people has become so strong that it continues to be part of the corporate way of life.

Whatever you think of the "resume first" policy of personnel managers, you have little choice in the matter. I have had applicants make very lengthy and logical arguments against the system—and I agreed with many of them—but there is no point in trying to understand the reasons for writing a resume. The best reason is that employers demand it.

Getting back to my demoralized applicant, I could not blame him for being disillusioned. His experience was typical of that which many job hunters go through. As difficult as it is to justify the endless request for resumes when all an applicant wants is an opportunity to sell himself in person to an employer, they do serve legitimate purposes.

What Do Resumes Accomplish?

Here are some of the things a resume does for both the employer and job seeker:

From the Employer's Standpoint

(1) By screening out the completely unqualified applicant, employers can give more time to the applicant whose resume contains at least some of the qualifications for the position. If resumes were completely eliminated and every applicant was granted an immediate interview, the truly qualified candidate would have to wait his turn while long, in-depth interviews were conducted with unqualified applicants. This would be economically disastrous to the job seekers and a waste of valuable time to the employer.

(2) By studying a resume in advance of an interview, the personnel manager has an opportunity to familiarize himself with the applicant's educational and work background. This eliminates a lot of preliminary questioning and probing when the applicant arrives, and saves time for both parties. The interviewer can better prepare for the personal meeting by knowing beforehand what clarification may be needed or where additional information is required.

(3) Many personnel people do only initial screening, and a resume is often passed up to the department that has the vacancy where the manager can review it. This, again, saves the time of the employer, insuring that only those who fit the job will be called in.

From the Applicant's Standpoint

(1) If you are called in for an interview on the basis of the information contained in your resume, and the personnel manager or department head is doing his job, you know that you must have at least some of the qualifications required. It is frustrating enough to look for employment without the additional discomfort of making unnecessary trips and waiting long hours for interviews that prove unfruitful because you were completely unqualified for the position.

(2) Preparing a resume requires you to dig into your past. Putting the facts on paper requires you to think about them, and this often reveals hidden strengths and weaknesses that you might ordinarily not be aware of. For this reason alone, even if a resume were not required, I would recommend that every job hunter make one. Putting yourself on paper for the first time may be a strain on your ego, but in the end it will improve your chances for a job.

(3) Resumes make the task of answering help wanted advertisements much simpler. Think of all the time and work involved if you had to compose a lengthy letter of application for every ad you answered, describing your background, education, and all the other information that would be required.

(4) Having a resume helps you organize your presentation. While you are talking about yourself at an interview you can follow the chronology of the resume and avoid jumping around, losing the continuity of your work experience, and missing important points. It will also help you remember dates and names.

(5) During an interview, a resume saves both you and the interviewer time. As a fact sheet, it eliminates the need to answer a lot of preliminary questions and leaves more time for the more important aspects of the interview.

(6) A resume keeps you honest. Under the pressure of an interview, you might be tempted to exaggerate a little here and there to enhance your image. Knowing that your interviewer is already aware of everything about you eliminates this temptation.

A Resume Checklist

As you study the sample resumes in later chapters, you will see that there are several different forms. The particular form you use is designed to present your qualifications in the strongest light and will depend upon your individual background. However, examination of each resume will reveal that the information it contains is basically the same. Every resume, no matter what its shape or format, must include certain pertinent information. Keep the following checklist before you at all times when you get down to actually putting your resume on paper. Each item is important.

(1) Personal identification
Name
Address
Phone number

(2) Title of position you are seeking or your objective

(3) Experience
Inclusive dates of your employment
Names and addresses of your employers
Your job title
Description of your duties and accomplishments

(4)   Education
Name of college or university
Dates of attendance
Degrees and honors achieved

(5)   Miscellaneous Information
Professional organizations and associations
References (optional)

The following items should never be included:

Religion or church affiliations
Race
Color
Age
National origin
Political preferences
Previous salaries
Anticipated salary
Reasons for leaving previous positions
Opinions of previous employers

Chapter 2
FORMAT AND MAKE-UP

While studying a resume, I sometimes try to visualize the physical appearance of the writer, not so much from his age, height, weight, or other indicated physical characteristics, but from the appearance of his resume: how it is organized, the quality of the printing, its neatness and cleanliness, how it is spaced on the page, the correctness of the grammar, spelling, and the general appearance. Then I compare my impression with his actual appearance and personality when he comes in to see me.

The two impressions don't always coincide. Prejudging an applicant only on the appearance of his resume may be unfair, but experienced personnel managers subconsciously do this and find that the appearance of the resume more often than not reflects the quality of the applicant.

I am not advocating a new science of personality evaluation, but I have found that flamboyant resumes often bring in overaggressive applicants; soiled, sloppy resumes with misspellings and general disorganization often bring in people whose backgrounds and personalities match their resumes.

This is not always the case, but it occurs often enough so that personnel people tend to gauge a person by his resume.

Flamboyant Resumes Flunk

The appearance and the format of your resume is almost as important as the information it contains. No matter how talented you are or how well you fit the job specifications, a physically unattractive resume, or one with elaborate embellishments, multi-colored inks, intricate folds, or on odd-sized paper can stop a potential interview in its tracks.

No one wants to squelch your individuality, but the resume is not the place to express your independence. The unorthodox presentation will surely attract attention, but is it the kind you want? Business people are generally conservative and any radical change from the norm upsets them. If you are as great as you think you are, wait until you get into an interview to prove it. Do not destroy your chances of getting that interview by showing off in your resume.

There are a few exceptions. Applicants for very creative jobs can use an unorthodox resume to highlight their talents. For instance, artists, designers, and writers can be more creative in their resumes, but again, within bounds. The point is, employers are generally looking for an individual who fits into a structured position, which has specific requirements such as experience, education, duties, and salary range. These are tangible ingredients which should be reflected in a resume. So long as you stick to these items you are on safe ground. A radical departure from the accepted norm at this stage of the game is dangerous and usually fruitless.

Reproduction

Here are some of the specifications to guide you in preparing your resume.
The only size that is acceptable is 8½ by 11 inches. If the size of your resume is

smaller or larger, it will undoubtedly stand out above the crowd, but it may cause you other problems. Most filing cabinets are built to accept letter-size documents. Business people and file clerks are conditioned by tradition and experience to handle 8½ × 11 inch sheets of paper. Anything which varies from that size can be a source of annoyance, and it is not beyond the realm of possibility that a clerk may just toss it into the wastebasket because it doesn't fit the file.

Contrary to some opinions, it is perfectly permissible to have a resume reproduced on a copier, provided that the copies are of high resolution on good bond paper. If you have access to a computer or word processor and a good-quality laser printer, by all means create and print out a professional-looking resume. However, a neatly typewritten resume is equally acceptable except, perhaps, for a high-level executive position. At one time, a personnel manager might have been horrified if he received one which was not typewritten. The theory was that if an applicant mass-produced his resume, he was obviously sending it out to every company in sight, and this was somehow considered unethical. Personnel managers no longer boggle at printed resumes and, in fact, the pendulum has swung the other way. I have had personnel managers tell me that they did not like typewritten resumes because it seemed that the applicant was tailoring his resume to fit the job he was applying for—as if there was something wrong with that. In reality, it does not matter whether your resume is individually typed or printed, so long as it contains the right information and conforms to accepted physical standards.

Commercial Resume Services

Wherever you live, there are probably resume preparation services available. They can be located in your telephone book and many of them advertise in local newspapers. These firms offer two kinds of services. One is an elaborate and often expensive service that also includes consultation and analysis of your background. Prices for this kind of service can run from fifty to several hundred dollars.

The other kind of resume service is a design, input, and printout service where they create a neat resume with the information you provide and reproduce any number of copies you desire.

With this book, you should be able to construct a resume equal to one that a high-priced resume service can produce.

Chapter 3

YOUR PERSONAL ASSESSMENT INVENTORY

As a job hunter, you are really in business for yourself. You are your own chief executive and the chief salesperson. You also have the distinction of being the product. Your objective is to put yourself out of business as soon as possible by selling out your stock.

Before you run out to call on your prospective customers you have to know what you are selling, the condition of your merchandise, and the price you want for it. In case you did not already know it, you are also the inventory manager and the controller of your business.

Your first step is to take a personal inventory. You may be a well-packaged product, but you consist of many parts and they have to be listed so that you know what to present to a buyer. An inventory fact sheet is absolutely necessary to have before you actually begin to make your resume. It will prevent your leaving out anything of importance, and will help you build the resume in a clear, organized way.

Know Your Strengths and Weaknesses

Before you write a resume, it is essential that you have before you a complete and detailed summary of your education and experience. You should be aware of your aptitudes, abilities, strengths, and weaknesses, and have a general idea of your objectives.

On the following pages are two questionnaires. The first, Your Personal Assessment Inventory, will provide you with a personal and professional profile which will show both your positive and negative attributes. If you are completely honest in answering the questions, you will be in a position to write a resume that will reflect only your strongest selling points.

The second questionnaire, the Resume Fact Sheet, is designed to insure that you don't omit any important facts from your resume. When you have completed it, the fact sheet will provide a handy guide to follow in writing the final draft of your resume.

Your Personal Assessment Inventory

Education

In which high school or college courses did you excel?

_____

_____

_____

In which courses did you do poorly?

_____

_____

_____

Which subjects did you enjoy most?

_____

_____

_____

Which subjects were tedious and boring? Why?

_____

_____

_____

If you are seeking employment in a field not directly related to your education, how do you think you can compensate for the lack of specialized training? _____

_____

_____

_____

Are you willing to continue your studies in order to increase your knowledge of the field you have chosen? _____

_____

_____

_____

What extra adult education courses have you taken? List the subjects and describe them. _____

_____

_____

_____

List any schooling you have had aside from your formal education. _____

_____

_____

_____

Did you participate in extracurricular activities? Describe your functions and accomplishments. _____

_____

_____

_____

Employment

Is your work experience spotty? If so, why did you change jobs often? _____

_____

_____

Have you ever been fired? Was it your fault? If so, what were the circumstances? ___

_____

_____

In which duties did you excel? Explain. _____

_____

_____

_____

What effect do you think the above will have on the type of job you are seeking? _____

_____

_____

_____

Which job-related activities do you do best? Explain. _____

_____

_____

_____

List any part-time jobs you have held while in school or after graduation. Describe your

duties. _____

_____

_____

_____

Aptitudes and Interests

List all of your skills (office machines, computer training, mechanical, artistic, creative,

etc.). _____

_____

_____

_____

Were these skills fully utilized in previous positions? _____

_____

_____

_____

What are your hobbies and personal interests? List everything, whether or not relevant

to your work or career. _____

_____

_____

_____

Which, if any, of the previous do you think has application to the kind of work you are seeking? _____

_____

_____

_____

What organizations have you been or are you now associated with? List technical, professional, or community groups. _____

_____

_____

_____

Are any members of the above groups in a position to help you in your job search? List them for future contacts. _____

_____

_____

_____

Achievements

What have been your main achievements (in school, job, or personal activities)? _____

_____

_____

How can you relate these achievements to your job hunt? _____

_____

_____

Describe any research papers, reports, or presentations you prepared. _____

_____

_____

_____

Describe any job-related decisions or recommendations that you made which resulted in more efficient operation of your department. _____

_____

_____

_____

What special recognition or awards did you receive either in school or on the job? ___

_____

_____

_____

List your promotion and salary record for each job you have held._____

_____

_____

_____

Describe your volunteer activities, such as fundraising, organizing, or social work. ___

_____

_____

_____

Miscellaneous

What kind of work would you really prefer to do? List *all* of your preferences, no matter how unrelated to your education or experience. _____

_____

_____

_____

Is salary your primary consideration? Would you sacrifice income to do the kind of work you most enjoy? Explain your feelings on this subject. _____

_____

_____

_____

Resume Fact Sheet

Provide all the information requested. Although some of the information asked for will not be included in your resume, complete each section fully. It may be useful in recalling information when preparing for an interview.

_____

Education

High School

Name of school _____

Location _____

Dates of attendance   from _____

                                       to _____

Description of courses (general, commercial, vocational)_____

_____

Subjects in which you excelled _____

_____

_____

Organizations and extracurricular activities _____

_____

Jobs held during summer vacations _____

_____

_____

College

Name of college or university _____

_____

Address _____

_____

Dates of attendance   from _____

                                       to _____

Major subjects _____

_____

Minor subjects _____

_____

Grade point average

_____   _____
          (major)   (overall)

Extracurricular activities, professional fraternities or sororities, organizations, study

groups, etc. _____

_____

_____

Work-study programs, internships, school jobs, etc. _____

_____

_____

_____

_____

Honors, awards, special citations _____

_____

Special achievements (academic, sports, hobby, personal) _____

_____

_____

_____

Additional Education   (Include all training—postgraduate, college, business, trade or

technical schools, military or corporate training programs. Include name of school, dates

of attendance, courses, degrees, or diplomas.) _____

_____

_____

_____

Work Experience

List your last position first. Include all of your duties and responsibilities.

Inclusive dates of employment _____ to _____

Title of your position _____

Company _____

Address _____

Company's function—products or services _____

_____

Description of your duties _____

_____

_____

Accomplishments (increase in department efficiency, cost savings, increased sales, new systems and procedures, etc.) _____

_____

_____

_____

_____

Inclusive dates of employment _____ to _____

Title of your position _____

Company _____

Address _____

Company's function—products or services _____

_____

Description of your duties _____

_____

_____

Accomplishments (increase in department efficiency, cost savings, increased sales, new systems and procedures, etc.) _____

_____

_____

Inclusive dates of employment _____ to _____

Title of your position _____

Address _____

Company's function—products or services _____

_____

Description of your duties _____

_____

_____

_____

_____

Accomplishments (increase in department efficiency, cost savings, increased sales, new

systems and procedures, etc.) _____

_____

_____

_____

_____

_____

Inclusive dates of employment _____ to _____

Title of your position _____

Company _____

Address _____

Company's function—products or services _____

_____

Description _____

_____

_____

_____

_____

Accomplishments (increase in department efficiency, cost savings, increased sales, new systems and procedures, etc.) _____

_____

_____

_____

_____

Skills and Abilities

List all of your special skills, such as office machines, computer knowledge, stenography, mathematics, technical, art—whether as a professional, hobbyist, or student.

_____

_____

_____

Miscellaneous

Membership in business or professional organizations. _____

_____

_____

_____

Are you willing to relocate? _____

Travel? _____

References

It is generally only necessary to state on your resume that references are available. A long list of references won't work to your advantage; in fact, it will most likely be considered superfluous.

Chapter 4

TYPES OF RESUMES

The variety of resumes crossing a busy personnel desk is infinite. There are short ones and long ones, cute ones and straightforward ones, clear ones and illegible ones. There are even resumes without names and addresses.

They come handwritten, typewritten, photocopied, and dittoed. Some are too short, providing no pertinent information; others read like autobiographies. But successful resumes—those that get job interviews—fall into only two basic categories: chronological and functional.

A good many resumes are rejected not because the applicant lacks the qualifications for the job, but because the reader can't find the information he wants in the plethora of words. Thus, it is vital that your resume take one of the above forms. The choice is determined by what you have to put into it, and this book will help you decide which is the best form for you.

What Must Go Into Your Resume

Each type of resume described here contains the same basic data, although each is arranged differently. This information falls into five distinct categories. They are:

  (1) Identification
  (2) Title of position desired or objective
  (3) Experience
  (4) Education
  (5) Miscellaneous information

Unless your resume includes each of these items, you will probably leave out some important information. A survey of personnel managers has shown that they find it much easier to extract the pertinent facts when the headings are in the order listed above. A resume that rambles or is disorganized probably will go into either a hold basket, or worse, into a wastebasket.

Let's look at the kind of information you provide under each heading. For the purpose of illustration, we will begin with the chronological form. Refer to the sample resumes beginning on page 26.

The Chronological Resume

Identification

At the top of the first page, write your name, address, and telephone number. Incredible as it may seem, resumes without a name or address are not uncommon. This is inexcusable carelessness, yet the writer may not realize the omission, even while waiting patiently for replies that never arrive.

Telephone numbers are absolutely necessary. Many busy executives prefer to pick up the telephone to make an appointment rather than write a letter. The extra delay, caused by the absence of your telephone number, can put you at the end of the line for an interview.

Title or Objective

This is actually the headline of your resume. Like its counterpart newspaper story, it should tell the reader in a few well-chosen words what to expect from the material which follows. Its importance cannot be overemphasized. The morning mail received by personnel offices contains resumes for many positions to be filled in the company and for your resume to be considered, it has to be matched against a specific opening. If your title or objective does not appear, or if it does not accurately reflect your background and experience, or the position you are seeking, it may not receive immediate action and may be relegated to a later reading.

The title or objective should appear, by itself, directly below your identification, centered and in capital letters or underscored.

How do you choose your job title? It is a simple matter if you are a specialist and your objective is singular and clear-cut.

For instance, if you are a Purchasing Agent, these two words are sufficient. The same thing applies if you are an Economist, Editor, Accountant, Programmer, or Bookkeeper to name just a few standard job titles.

Titles Can Be Tricky

Not all titles fit so snugly, however, and many require more thought. For instance, if you are in personnel, there are many facets to your work. You can be a manager or an assistant. You may be in wage and salary administration or industrial relations. There are training specialists, interviewers, and recruiters, and many combinations of all of these specialties. Here are some of the titles which can be used in the personnel category.

Human Resources Director
Industrial Relations Manager
Director of Personnel
College Recruiter
Personnel Assistant
Wage and Salary Administrator
Benefits Manager
Personnel Trainee

Another example is advertising. You can be an advertising copywriter, advertising production assistant or manager, advertising media buyer, traffic manager, or account executive. Just using the word "advertising" is not enough for your prospective employer to evaluate the work which you can do. Study the sample resumes for other examples.

A special word must be added about a much abused and misused term—Administrative Assistant. Unless it can be made more specific, the term, used by itself, identifies the applicant as an office worker, and can include anything from a secretary to a department manager.

An administrative assistant in the engineering department of a television set manufacturer is a far cry from an administrative assistant in the admissions office of a hospital, or an administrative assistant to a controller. Secretaries are often referred to as Administrative Assistants. If, however, you must use the term, be sure you relate it to your experience. Otherwise, you may remain titled, but without visible means of support. For example:

Administrative Assistant to Sales Manager
Administrative Assistant to Publisher
Administrative Assistant—Order Dept.

Education

The longer you have been away from your formal schooling, the less important are the details. However, it is necessary to list at least the name of the college you attended, inclusive dates, and degrees earned. If you are a fairly recent graduate, you should elaborate somewhat, stating your major course of study and other details that you feel are relevant to the job you seek. List all supplementary education you may have received in other schools, including night and correspondence courses and any business-related courses.

Discretion, Not Deception

Although you should never lie about your education, discretion is sometimes advisable. Giving too much information can be harmful. For instance, if you are seeking a position in business, and you majored in Drama and Theater, Medieval Japanese Literature, or Classical Greek, it is sufficient to simply state that you graduated with a BA, and leave out the title of your major subject, unless, of course it has a direct bearing on your qualifications for the job you seek. On the other hand, if you are applying for a job in publishing and you have an MS in journalism, be sure it is not only stated, but underscored. From the point of view of your resume, you have to determine which portion of your education is an asset to you and which could be a possible liability—and arrange the emphasis accordingly. Remember, the purpose of a resume is to create a favorable climate for your interview. It is not necessary to confess everything until you are asked.

Experience

This is the "hard sell" portion of your resume, the section which tells a prospective employer what you have done for others, and therefore, what you can do for him.

The major difference between the two resumes—chronological and functional— is in the arrangement and explanation of your experience. Since we are discussing the chronological resume, let us see how your experience is handled.

Simply stated, the chronological resume lists your jobs in reverse order, with the last first. This allows the reader to track your career back from your present or last job to your first. Also, most personnel people are used to seeing resumes in this last-to-first order and a departure from this form can confuse the reader.

Each item in the experience section of your resume must contain the following information:

(1) Inclusive dates of employment
(2) Name and address of company
(3) What the company makes or what service it performs
(4) Title of your position
(5) Description of your duties
(6) Accomplishments—what you did that was noteworthy

Let us consider each of these items separately and see how we can put this section together.

(1) *Dates of employment:* Month and year are sufficient. If you are still employed, use the words "March, 1983 to present." Do not skip any positions because you feel they were not relevant or too short in duration. Every period of your time must be accounted for, except gaps between jobs. However, even in this instance, if you have such gaps of at least six months' duration or more, be prepared to explain your activities in your interview. Long periods of unaccounted-for time on a resume always raise questions.

(2) *Name and address of company:* State the full name of the company. If the firm is a subsidiary of a larger one, indicate the name of the parent company. Be sure the address is complete, including street number. Do not just say "Rawlings Corporation, Philadelphia, Pa." When the time comes to check references, the full address of your previous firm will be needed.

(3) *What the company does:* Describe the products the firm manufactures or the service it performs. You may be familiar with what your firm does, but unless it is one of the well-known companies, its function may not be apparent in its name. A short description such as "Manufacturers of precision electronic parts" or "Importers of heavy machinery" will be sufficient to give the reader some idea of what kind of business you were involved with.

(4) *Title of your position:* If you had more than one, list your main title, followed by any secondary ones. Don't attempt to describe your position in the title. Simple terms such as "Production Manager" or "Assistant to Controller" will suffice.

(5) *Description of your duties:* In simple language, describe the functions you performed. For example: "Supervised four assistants in the production and booking of public service films. Distributed films to major television stations. Performed media research"—or—"I handled all aspects of production, wrote specifications, established pricing policy, planned production, and issued purchase orders."

In describing your duties be brief and do not overstate your job. The real sales pitch is in the paragraph following the description of your duties.

(6) *Accomplishments—what you did that was noteworthy:* Many resumes come in with just the dates of employment, the title of the position, and a list of duties. These facts tell a reader little about your competence on the job, but this section allows you to expand a bit on your own talents, and how you used them in the job you are describing. In looking back over your career with a company you may find it difficult to recall just what accomplishments stand out in the daily routine of business. Of course, not everyone makes great contributions, but diligent performance of your duties, even in the most routine job, adds to the general well-being of the firm.

For example, if you were in an accounting job, you could list the systems and procedures you instituted to improve the operation of your department. As a purchasing assistant you may have saved the firm money by helping to develop new sources of supply. Perhaps you were an administrative assistant to a sales manager. There must have been areas where you tightened up the paper work or improved the record-keeping and order systems. Were you in a supervisory position? Indicate how many people you supervised. List the titles of the executives to whom you were responsible. If your job was creative or required writing skills, be sure to mention this. There is a broad appreciation—and need for—people with good abilities to communicate clearly all through industry, and the person who can write clearly has a distinct advantage over his competition in a job hunt. Tell about your additional responsibilities, promotions, and awards that came along. A word of caution: do not boast. You don't want to be so good that you will overqualify yourself.

Age

Despite federal, state, and local legislation, age discrimination still exists. If you believe you have been turned down because of your age, you have the right to seek legal redress. But how do you know? It's no secret that many companies still discriminate, using subtle (and not so subtle) reasons to refuse to hire a suitable job applicant. Whether you have just graduated from school or are over 45, your age or date of birth should *never* appear on your resume. Even in the interview, employers are not permitted by law to ask how old applicants are.

Miscellaneous Information

(1) Professional organizations and associations
(2) References

(1) *Professional organizations and associations:* Extracurricular activities can enhance your credentials. List any trade or professional associations you belong to, but not political or religious ones.

(2) *References:* As a general rule, references need not appear on a resume. Whether you state that they will be provided upon request or hold them for the interview, references are part of your personal and professional record and when they are needed for checking, they should be available.

Your references should be chosen very carefully. Many applicants, through ignorance or carelessness, count on references that are, at the very least, shaky. Never take a previous employer for granted. It is always a good idea, when you are looking for a job, to telephone your selected references and tell them that their names will be supplied on request in your job interviews. This is a good procedure for two reasons. First, if your prospective references have been alerted to the fact that they will be receiving inquiries, they are likely to respond more quickly to them. Second, your call will confirm that the individual you are naming as a reference is still with your old firm. If he is not, the inquiry may go to someone who does not know you personally. Also, your call to a former employer may evoke a warmer response when the reference inquiry does arrive.

Are You Sure of Your References?

Choose your references carefully. In supplying a reference be sure to name the person in the firm who you are certain will give you a favorable report. Even though you may have performed your duties competently, there might be someone in the firm with whom you did not get along. If so, and you know it, keep the name to yourself. Many a job has been lost because an applicant provided a reference without being certain that it would be a good one. If you have any suspicion that an individual in your previous company might not be on your side, pick another.

If you left your previous employment under less than ideal circumstances, and you know that your reference at best will be a cool one, you are on the spot.

You cannot leave out the reference completely since you probably have listed the firm as a former employer. But you can attempt to repair the damage.

The only way to do this, however, is to telephone the person for whom you worked and tell him or her you hope he will give you a favorable report. If, for any reason, you cannot do this, or are sure that you are stuck with a bad report, try to work it out at the interview.

At that time, tell your prospective employer frankly what the circumstances surrounding your separation were and that you are not certain of your references. This at least, gives you a fighting chance—it is much better to handle the situation this way than to knowingly give a reference which could turn out to be questionable.

Get the Reference Before You Leave

It is a good idea, when leaving a position, to request that a letter of reference be given to you before your departure. Having a satisfactory reference in your possession can eliminate any problem due to changes in personnel in your former company. Once you have a reference, it is unlikely that your employer would have second thoughts about your competence should he receive an inquiry from one of your prospective employers.

Which Resume Is Best For You?

There are two basic types of resumes—chronological and functional.

In the first, you list your employment by date with your last job shown first, followed by a description of your duties. The functional resume emphasizes your responsibilities and accomplishments, rather than the dates and the amount of time you spend in each job.

Which type is best for you to use depends upon your individual work history and background. By checking the appropriate boxes for each type, you will be able to determine which one will do the best job for you.

Chronological Resume
Should be used if:

☐ You have spent three or more years with previous employers and have not changed jobs frequently.

☐ You are seeking a position in the same field in which you have been employed during the course of your career.

☐ You have worked for prestigious companies that are well-known.

☐ You can show steady growth in responsibilities and salary.

☐ Your references are impeccable.

Functional Resume
Should be used if:

☐ You are seeking a job in a new field not related to your present career.

☐ You are reentering the job market after a long absence.

☐ You have been unemployed for more than three months.

☐ Your present salary is below average for your age and experience.

☐ Your duties and responsibilities are complicated and require explanation.

☐ You can point to specific accomplishments while on your last two jobs.

☐ You have an age problem, having to compete with younger applicants for the same level positions.

Power Verbs

Choose action verbs whenever possible to describe your duties and responsibilities.

A

activated
actuated
addressed
administered
advised
analyzed
arbitrated
arranged
assembled
assisted
attracted
audited
authored

B

built

C

calculated
charted
closed up
collected
compiled
completed
composed
compounded
conceived
concluded
conducted
confined
conserved
consolidated
constructed
consulted
contracted
contributed
controlled
coordinated
corrected
corresponded
counseled
created
criticized

D

decreased
delivered
demonstrated
designed
detected
determined
developed

devised
diagnosed
diagrammed
directed
disciplined
discovered
dispensed
disproved
disseminated
distributed
documented
doubled
drew up

E

edited
eliminated
enhanced
enlarged
established
evaluated
examined
exceeded
executed
expanded
expedited

F

facilitated
forecasted
formulated
funneled
founded

G

guided

H

headed

I

identified
illuminated
illustrated
implemented
improved
increased
initiated
innovated
interpreted
installed
instituted
instructed

introduced
invented
investigated
interviewed

L

launched
lectured
logged

M

maintained
managed
maximized
minimized
modernized
modified
motivated

N

navigated
negotiated

O

obtained
operated
optimized
ordered
organized
originated
overhauled
oversaw

P

performed
planned
prepared
prescribed
presented
procured
produced
promoted
processed
proposed
protected
provided
put together

R

realized
received
recommended

reconciled
recorded
recruited
reduced
refined
rendered
replaced
represented
researched
restored
reviewed
revised
revitalized
routed

S

safeguarded
secured
selected
served
shut down
simplified
slashed
sold
solved
sparked
staffed
started
stimulated
studied
summarized
supervised
supplied
synthesized
systemized

T

terminated
tested
took charge
took over
trained
transacted
translated
triggered

U

upgraded

V

verified

W

wrote

Sample Resumes — Chronological Form

JOHN A. RAWLINGS
133 Pine Avenue
Ridgefield, NJ 07932
(201) 555-2376

PERSONNEL ADMINISTRATION/INDUSTRIAL RELATIONS

OBJECTIVE   To join an organization where I can use my skills and expertise in personnel administration and attain a high level of performance in personnel recruitment, training, and administration.

EXPERIENCE

Sept. 1986
to
Present

Allied Manufacturing Corporation
325 Lexington Avenue
New York, NY 10022

Position: Personnel Director
Duties: Administer the formal personnel policy program; supervise the policy committee; administer the benefit program including pension and medical insurance. Establish recruiting procedures; supervise interviewers and maintain liaison between department managers and the personnel department.

Advise management on manpower forecasting and budget control; participate in high-level policy meetings on performance review and incentive programs.

Establish wage and salary standards; maintain current statistics on the labor market and company's competitive standing.

Supervise training programs; administer workman's compensation; oversee compliance with all governmental employment regulations, and affirmative action programs.

Feb. 1980
to
Sept. 1986

Northeast Aircraft Corporation
14 Arlington Road
Trenton, NJ 07823

Position: Assistant Personnel Manager
Duties: Reported directly to the personnel manager in personnel administrative functions at division level. The personnel department with both line and staff authority consisted of 10 people. During this time, sales growth of the company from 1 million to 35 million dollars required the addition of over 500 employees.

Responsible for the recruitment of all exempt employees earning from $18,000 to $50,000 per year in the marketing, sales, financial, and administrative areas. Also participated in the non-exempt employment program.

Assisted the personnel manager in all areas of wage and salary administration, performance review procedures, job descriptions, and evaluation programs.

Continued...

June 1977 to Jan. 1980	**Buyers Discount Stores, Inc.** Cherry Hill Shopping Centers, Inc. Cherry Hill, NJ 07982

Position: Personnel Assistant
Duties: Reported directly to the employment manager of this large discount department store of 800 employees. Handled general employment functions including promotions, placements, and reductions in force in accordance with union agreement.

Was promoted to supervisor of clerical employment and was responsible for personnel administration of 24 clerks in the front office.

1976 to 1977	Previous employment of one year with private trade school as general office assistant. Miscellaneous duties consisted of routine office work, typing, filing, and general record keeping.

EDUCATION	**University of California, Davis,** CA Graduated 1975 — B.S. in Management

University of Pennsylvania, Philadelphia, PA
Evening courses in Personnel Administration

American Management Association
Special seminar courses in labor relations, contract negotiation, and wage and salary administration.

WILLING TO RELOCATE

REFERENCES AVAILABLE UPON REQUEST

MARTHA RESNICK
1463 Hollingdale Avenue
New Brunswick, NJ 07475
(201) 555-4856

OBJECTIVE: To obtain a position as a programmer in business applications, leading to management.

HARDWARE USED: IBM 360/65
IBM 370/168
IBM 3350 disk and mass storage system
IBM 3278 CRT's

SOFTWARE KNOWLEDGE: Cobol, Assembler, PL/I, Fortran, JCL, Timesharing, Structured Programming, ISAM, VSAM.

WORK EXPERIENCE:
1987-Present

Savage Industries, Inc.
Elizabeth, New Jersey

Programmer — Responsibilities include application programming, statistical quality control, program design and implementation, debugging, maintenance, language conversion, and microfiche conversion.

EDUCATION:
1985

Fairleigh Dickinson University
Rutherford, New Jersey

B.S. Mathematics. Major studies include:
• Statistical Math Applications
• Introduction to Computers
• Structured Programming

1987

New Jersey State Technical Institute
Newark, New Jersey

Computer Science. Major studies include:
• Programming
• Operating Systems
• Database Management Systems

MISCELLANEOUS: Member of: **American Association of Programmers**
Statistical Society of New Jersey
Automated Systems Association
Association for Women in Computing

Bernice Stern
235 East 19th Street
Boston, MA 02134
(617) 555-5687

<u>Bookkeeper</u>

Education:

Benjamin Franklin High School
Boston, MA

Commercial Courses:
- Bookkeeping
- Typing
- Gregg Shorthand
- Commercial Law
- Economics
- Word Processing

Experience:

1989 to 1993

Fremont & Company, Inc.
121 Knorr Street
Boston, MA

Full-charge bookkeeper, through general ledger. Payroll for 120 people. Prepared tax reports, maintained accounts receivable and accounts payable ledgers.

1988 to 1989

Herbert Real Estate, Inc.
1416 Barclay Avenue
Boston, MA

Assistant bookkeeper and secretary. Posted accounts receivables and payables, reconciled bank statements, kept petty cash records. Secretary to the chief accountant.

1986 to 1988

Weissman & Smith, CPAs
980 W. 21st Street
Boston, MA

Assistant bookkeeper. Maintained clients' books, including taxes, payroll, and bank reconciliations. Assisted accountants in making up financial reports. Typed letters and did general clerical duties.

1982 to 1986

National Shipping Company
Boston, MA

As part of a 4-person office, helped prepare payroll for 35 employees. Assisted the head bookkeeper; filled in as switchboard operator and did general clerical and typing duties.

Skills:

Type—55 words per minute
Steno—90 words per minute
Knowledge NCR 5500 bookkeeping machine

RANDOLPH R. FOREST
41 MASSACHUSETTS AVENUE
SPRINGFIELD, MA 02136
(617) 555-4398

**HEALTH CARE ADMINISTRATION
AND MANAGEMENT**

EDUCATION:

1985   **MS in Public Health Administration**
University of Massachusetts, Boston, MA

1975   **BS in Psychology**
Boston University, Boston, MA

EXPERIENCE:

1986-Present   **Managing Director**
Robert P. Lorimer Clinic, Springfield, MA

Responsible for the operation of the entire facility, including financial planning, cost control, marketing, and personnel. Coordinate nursing, surgical, and medical activities.

• Administer an annual budget of $3 million. Increased profits the first year and maintained steady growth of income thereafter.

• Developed marketing plan to private agencies and physicians which resulted in increased referrals from these sources.

• Instituted a public affairs program to acquaint the community with the services available from the clinic. This resulted in an appreciable increase in the number of people using the facility.

• Was responsible for instituting changes in third-party reimbursement procedures which resulted in more efficient billing practices.

1984-1986   **Assistant Director**
Forsgate Hospital, Providence, RI

Responsibilities included managing medical records department, inpatient and outpatient admittance, utilization review, and budget planning. Supervised staff of 135.

1981-1984   **Administrative Supervisor**
John H. Ryder Psychiatric Clinic, Providence, RI

Full responsibility for management of 55-bed unit. Administered all areas, including educational, therapeutic, and emergency services. Was also involved with personnel training, program development, and staff hiring.

Continued...

• Instituted new cost procedures which reduced budget by 12 percent.

• Installed new billing and collection system which increased cash flow by 15 percent.

• Served on Board of Directors and participated in major decision-making meetings.

1975-1980   **Instructor in Psychology**
Boston University, Boston, MA

AFFILIATIONS: American Public Health Association
American Management Association
American Academy of Hospital Administrators
Association of Psychiatric Clinics

REFERENCES ON REQUEST

Sandra Larch

821 Ohio Street   •   Bryn Mawr, PA 19010   •   (215) 555-5833

Objective: A position in corporate communications with emphasis on writing and editing employee publications and external house organs.

Summary of Qualifications: Fifteen years' experience in written communications, including public relations, magazine and newspaper writing, editing, layout, and production. Responsibilities and assignments have included the writing of articles on business practices, interviewing, reporting of meetings and conventions, and the compete production of internal and external house organs, employee bulletins, and manuals. Other skills includes promotional writing, product publicity, and direct mail advertising.

Experience:

June 1982-Present

CLAWSON COLLEGE, Lancaster, Pennsylvania
Assistant Public Relations Manager — Function of PR department is to provide communications, publications, and programs to support alumni relations and student recruitment. Duties are to write and supervise production of newsletters and internal employee publications. This includes news features for alumni magazines, news releases for local and national media, and supervision of printing. Also plan and execute special projects, including membership drives and special events.

April 1979-June 1982

THE DAILY CHRONICLE, Buffalo, New York
Copyeditor and Reporter — Started with this newspaper of 85,000 daily circulation as copyeditor and rewrite editor. Promoted to general assignment reporter, covering local news. In addition, wrote special features on such subjects as political campaigns, municipal problems, and local personalities. Was cited by the publisher for special investigative reporting of local hospital scandal.

January 1979-February 1981

AMERICAN BUSINESS PUBLISHING CO.
435 Chestnut Street, Philadelphia, Pennsylvania
Editorial Assistant — Duties with this trade magazine publisher included proofreading, copyediting, makeup, and production. Wrote heads, picture captions, and performed general editorial duties under the supervision of the managing editor.

Education:
1977

B.A. in English and American Literature
HAVERFORD COLLEGE, Haverford, Pennsylvania

1979

M.A. in Journalism
TEMPLE UNIVERSITY, Philadelphia, PA

While attending Haverford College, served as editor of the campus newspaper for one year and as assistant editor on the annual student magazine. At Temple, earned part of tuition by serving as part-time staff assistant to the University Public Relations Director. In this capacity, received valuable writing experience and a good knowledge of public relations procedures.

ALBERT DAVIS

1220 E. 63rd Street   Chicago, IL 60612   (312) 555-4732

SALES ADMINISTRATION
ADMINISTRATIVE SERVICES

EXPERIENCE
January 1984-
Present

ADMINISTRATIVE ASSISTANT TO VICE PRESIDENT, MARKETING
Universal Laboratories, Inc., 325 Madison Street, Chicago, IL

Serving in Fieldstone Division, leading producer of enzymes and specialty chemicals. Duties include:

- Supervision of sales-service staff covering both domestic and foreign operations.
- Liaison with banks, freight forwarders, government agencies, foreign consulates, factories, and regional warehouses.
- Handling and expediting orders requiring special attention.
- Processing and analysis of invoices and other data transmitted from foreign subsidiaries with subsequent preparation of monthly sales reports.
- Approving vendor invoices for payment and maintenance of local Imprest Bank account.
- Follow-up of delinquent accounts to resolve past-due and unexplained open items.
- Supervision of office services, including hiring of secretarial and clerical personnel.
- Preparation of annual and quarterly unit and dollar sales forecasts of domestic, Canadian, and export divisions.

December 1979-
November 1983

FIELD SERVICES ADMINISTRATOR
Zephyr Industries, Inc., 1850 Michigan Avenue, Chicago, IL

Principal responsibilities while serving in consumer products division included:

- Supervision of customer service operation.
- Providing support for field sales force with information and assistance in connection with orders, products, policies, and procedures.
- Processing dealer purchase contracts.
- Approving and processing cooperative advertising claims.
- Handling of special account orders and interdivisional company requisitions.

Continued...

October 1978-
November 1979

ADMINISTRATIVE ASSISTANT TO NATIONAL SALES MANAGER
RMC Corporation, 311 Parkside Avenue, Chicago, IL

Duties with one of the leading business equipment manufacturers essentially covered liaison functions between field operations and corporate headquarters.
- Contact with inventory control to determine proper levels
    for various models within consumer product line.
- Preparation of production schedules consistent with
    sales forecasts.
- Resolution of sales accounting items related to billing
    procedures and assignment of field sales credit.
- Working with advertising department in preparation
    of price lists and sales promotion material.
- Handling both dealer and end-user inquiries, particularly
    in connection with service problems.

January 1972-
November 1978

ASSISTANT SALES-SERVICE MANAGER
Universal Electronics Corporation, 6821 N. Falls Road, Peoria, IL

Responsibilities with this major electronics distributor of components and equipment included:
- Extensive correspondence, telephone contacts, and
    personal meetings with dealers, salesmen, consumers,
    and manufacturing personnel.
- Supervision of order processing and customer service
    departments.
- Assisting in the preparation of bulletins and sales
    promotion materials, showroom sales, and new
    product presentations.
- Planning and arranging exhibits at national and
    regional trade shows, with coordination of all
    activities, including sales meetings related to
    company participation.

EDUCATION:
1972

University of Chicago, Chicago, Illinois
Degree: B.A. — Liberal Arts

Postgraduate courses and seminars:
- Business Management and Organization —
    American Management Association
- Sales and Sales Promotion —
    Sales Executives Club
- Marketing and Distribution —
    National Advertisers Association

CATHERINE HODDES
3925 Market Street
Newark, N.J. 07102
(201) 555-9846

CREDIT/CUSTOMER SERVICE

EDUCATION:
1988-1989

Fairleigh Dickinson University
Rutherford, New Jersey

June 1988

Lincoln High School
Newark, New Jersey

EMPLOYMENT:

Haymar Fashion Jeans, Inc.
500 Seventh Avenue
New York, N.Y.

Assistant to the Customer Service Manager
Handled all correspondence for chain store accounts
concerning status of orders, return of merchandise,
issuing of credit or debit memos. Prepared reports
of shipments, deliveries and returns.

Inter-American Publishing Co.
1120 Avenue of the Americas
New York, N.Y.

Clerk in Credit Department
Worked on assigned individual accounts, issued credit
and debit memos. Wrote letters to customers regarding
unpaid bills. Handled telephone collections, typed memos
to department heads and performed general filing and
clerical duties.

SKILLS:

Type 50 words per minute
Operate the Wang 453 word processor

References on request

Bernard Cooper
5867 Arlington Avenue
Newark, N.J. 07104
(201) 555-6974

CHIEF STRUCTURAL ENGINEER

Objective: To join the management staff of an organization which can fully utilize the services of a Professional Engineer with 14 years' experience in all phases of precast-prestressed concrete plant operation including:

- Sales Promotion
- Estimating
- Product Design
- Plant & Equipment Design
- Drafting Room Supervision
- Quality Control

Experience:
1977-present   **Ranier Construction Co., Inc.**, 256 Main Street, Newburgh, New York.
- Supervise the Engineering Department and advise management on engineering problems.
- Prepare product cost studies and initiate preliminary design and layouts.
- Review engineering designs and details, supervise Engineering department personnel in the preparation of drawings and specifications for plant facilities and equipment, including cost and budget analysis.
- Maintain liaison with and advise manufacturing department on fabrication of product and new plant equipment and maintenance.
- Analyze Engineering Department personnel requirements, and prepare operating budgets.
- Set quality control standards and check product for compliance.
- Recruit, hire, train, and evaluate all Engineering personnel.
- Analyze operational procedures and perform time and motion studies to establish efficient systems for work-flow to the production department.

Additional Responsibilities:
Consultant to the president of the company on engineering, plans, specifications, and cost studies; work very closely with the sales manager as consultant and advisor in the effective promotion, design, and cost of the product; work in the field with architects, engineers, and subcontractors on structural problems and product application; work with accounting, credit, and legal departments in matters of engineering, product performance, and costs.

1971-1977   Architectural designer and engineer for various local design firms.

Education:
1970   **New Jersey State College of Engineering**, Newark, New Jersey
Bachelor of Science in Architectural Engineering

1971   **Drexel Institute**, Philadelphia, Pennsylvania
Advanced structural courses

**Professional
Associations:**   Registered Professional Engineer in Pennsylvania, Delaware, New Jersey, and New York.
Member of Prestressed Concrete Institute.

BERNICE COGIN

| 1922 Sadlier Road | Forest Hills, NY 11218 | (718) 555-9613 |

PRINTING PRODUCTION

CAREER OBJECTIVE

A position in which knowledge of graphic arts, photography, printing production, and purchasing would enhance job performance.

EXPERIENCE

April 1987
to
Present

BALLARD PRINTING COMPANY
625 Madison Avenue
New York, NY 19002

Estimator, New York Sales Office

Report to Sales Manager. Direct activities of assistant estimator. Responsible for all estimates, contracts, quotes, and commissions for six salesmen in busy New York sales office processing over 12 million dollars in printing sales per year. Took over estimating responsibilities to replace retiring chief estimator, preventing loss of several hundred thousand dollars in contracts. Conducted preliminary interviews and trained assistant estimator when increased volume due to increased competition from new companies in field required additional staff.

March 1985
to
January 1987

ALLIED REPRODUCTION CORPORATION
84 Varick Street
New York, NY 10018

Purchasing Agent

Reported directly to Director of Purchasing. Shared department function in purchasing of paper, stock, engravings, ink, and other necessary materials. Developed new purchase order record system which prevented duplication of payments. Enabled management to keep better track of back orders which had been overlooked previously.

May 1980
to
February 1985

AMERICAN BANK COMPANY
40 Wall Street
New York, NY 10016

Senior Remittance Clerk

Reported to Department Supervisor. Maintained records of trust accounts worth millions of dollars. Checked for accuracy and coordinated mailing of checks. Computed commissions and supervised assistant's performance.

Continued...

March 1978
to
April 1980

NATIONAL BANK OF NORTH AMERICA
120 Broadway
New York, NY 10016

Acceptance Clerk

Examined letters of credit for validity and acceptability.
Promoted four times in a two-year period to jobs of
increasing responsibility.

EDUCATION
1978

NEW YORK INSTITUTE OF PHOTOGRAPHY
New York, NY
Diploma in Modern Photography

HIGH SCHOOL OF PRINTING
New York, NY

**PROFESSIONAL
ASSOCIATIONS**

Member of Photographic Society of America
Member of New York Advertising Club
Member of Production Club of New York

ROBERT LATHROP
1104 Sagamore Street
Albany, N.Y. 12369
(518) 555-4865

OBJECTIVE
Sales/Marketing Engineering Manager for a high-technology corporation seeking an individual with advanced degrees in Engineering and Business, and experience in engineering, product development, and sales management.

EDUCATION
STATE UNIVERSITY OF NEW YORK, Albany, NY
M.S. — Mechanical Engineering

UNIVERSITY OF CHICAGO, Chicago, IL
M.B.A. — Business Management

DREXEL UNIVERSITY, Philadelphia, PA
B.S. — Aeronautical Engineering

EXPERIENCE
NORTHAMERICAN POWER COMPANY, Buffalo, New York — 1979 to present

Marketing Manager — Developed sales base for a foundry division. Supervised three engineers and two sales representatives. Created market strategy and sales budgets. Prepared quotations and pricing procedures. Estimated costs.

Developed bidding standards involving engineering, manufacturing, and quality control, resulting in an increase of new contracts won by the corporation in competitive bidding.

Sales Engineer — Organized sales force into teams consisting of technical and marketing specialists which resulted in an 18% increase in sales over a 2-year period. Developed a computerized follow-up system which measured performance and cost, resulting in eliminating over $325,000 cost overruns. Initiated standards for proposal presentations which eliminated excessive administrative costs.

Product Manager — Reported to Product Planning Manager. Responsible for the preparation of sales promotional material, pricing, and sales presentations.

Worked with market research department in determining potential new markets for the product line. Prepared a 150-page catalog for the use of sales engineers and customers.

Design Engineer — Assisted in the development of product improvement and new product lines. Initiated new plant procedures which reduced manufacturing costs by 20%.

Developed new maintenance system which cut man-hour requirements and reduced costs about 15% overall. Helped reorganize the engineering department to more effectively utilize personnel and equipment.

MISCELLANEOUS
- Registered Professional Engineer
- Member of American Society of Design Engineers, Association of Electrical Power Engineers, and New York State Engineering Society
- Instructor in Technical Writing at the University of New York at Albany
- Recipient of Engineering Management Award
- Willing to relocate or travel

Leonard Campbell
1325 Harrison Road
Cleveland, OH 31620
(216) 555-6835

Assistant Controller
Financial Analyst

Job Objective: To join the staff in the controller's office of a large corporation and to participate in the analysis of financial and economic problems with a view to developing appropriate courses of action.

Experience:
1986-present

Harmon-Harding Corporation
1235 Randolph Street, Cleveland, Ohio

Accounts Receivables Manager — Duties involve management of accounts receivable departments consisting of six employees. Substantial contact with customers, financial officers and close liaison with marketing departments. Knowledge of financial requirements of various industries served, and general business conditions required.

1984-1986

Lawrence Plastics Corporation
165 Main Street, Cleveland, Ohio

Junior Accountant — Duties involved analysis of financial position of customers. Required knowledge of techniques of financial statement analysis, and familiarity with accepted accounting principles. Assisted with cash management function and bank liaison.

1981-1984

Ohio Bank & Trust Company
Cleveland, Ohio

Credit Assistant — Involved in training program in commercial loan department. Responsible for analysis of accounts. Assisted credit manager.

Education:
1979-1981

Graduate School of Business Administration
University of Michigan, Ann Arbor, Michigan

Received a degree of Master of Business Administration in June 1981, concentrating in economics with strong preparation in finance and quantitative analysis.

Courses taken: Business Conditions, Analysis and Forecasting, Managerial Economics, Fundamentals of Accounting, International Trade and Finance, Theory of Financial Management, Matrix Algebra, Theory of Probability and Statistical Inference.

1974-1979

Ohio State University, Columbus, Ohio
Degree: Bachelor of Arts. *Major:* Accounting.
President of ROTC fraternity.

MICHAEL MORRISON
46 Felton Avenue
Ft. Lee, NJ 07036
(201) 555-2347

OFFICE MANAGER

SUMMARY
Over 17 years' experience in all phases of administration including supervisory and managerial positions. Responsibilities included management of clerical personnel, development and implementation of systems and procedures, and the maintenance of automated and manual inventory control and material management systems. Thorough knowledge of accounting and auditing procedures, automated warehousing systems, and office services.

EXPERIENCE
Store-Pak Industries, 1964 Clay Avenue, Bronx, New York (1986-Present)
Assistant Inventory Control Manager — Report to the Inventory Control Manager. Supervise all phases of inventory control and material management. Responsible for preparation and implementation of inventory control and material management systems and procedures, requirements planning, maintenance of an automated system, order processing and material procurement. (Annual volume $24 million) Direct and coordinate the inventory control section for maximum efficiency in all phases of operation.

Harrison Food Corporation, Orange, New Jersey (1984-1986)
Office Manager — Supervised 21 clerical employees. Responsible for all administrative functions including accounts payable and receivable, bookkeeping, work planning and scheduling, office systems, correspondence, forms design, and control. Functioned as Personnel Manager, Benefits Administrator, and Office Services Manager. Forecasted and prepared the annual administrative budget, established a wage and salary procedure and a salary review program. Arbiter of employment and wage regulations.

Madison Supermarkets, Inc., Secaucus, New Jersey (1972-1984)
Administrator and Senior Planner, Inventory Control — Supervised 21 employees in a computerized inventory control department. Responsible for the administration of an automated inventory control system. This included the acquisition, utilization, and disposal of all physical assets. Was also responsible for all computer application as well as system analysis and design. Created and developed automated and manual inventory control systems. Reviewed and continuously evaluated existing systems and procedures and wrote procedures and manuals covering inventory control, warehousing, requisitioning, purchasing, receiving, and shipping.

EDUCATION
New Jersey State University (Evening Division)
Punched Card Systems and Procedures

New York University
1 year — Business Management

REFERENCES
Available upon request

Jason Painter
61 Marsh Avenue
Stamford, CT 04072
(203) 555-6436

Personnel/Labor Relations Manager

Objective
Responsible management position utilizing personnel recruiting, labor relations, and administrative background and experience.

Experience
August 1982
to Present

Lamston, Storey, Inc. (Department Store Chain)
1841 Broadway, New York, New York

EXECUTIVE RECRUITER AND PERSONNEL MANAGER — Plan, establish, and conduct activities for the recruitment, screening, selection, and placement of all exempt employees for all branches. Maintain close liaison with all major graduate schools and colleges to insure a steady flow of highly qualified applicants. Supervise the maintenance and retention of employment files and records. Member of Middle Management Selection Committee.

October 1978 to
August 1982

Joseph Sorenson & Company
1694 Clayton Avenue, Bronx, New York

LABOR RELATIONS REPRESENTATIVE — Responsible for contract negotiations. Handled pre-arbitrations, wage and salary studies. Instituted a supervisor training program which resulted in reduction of turnover of plant management personnel.

April 1972 to
September 1978

Sweetland General Hospital
Elmira, New York

MANAGER OF PERSONNEL AND LABOR RELATIONS — Formulated and established an entire new department. Wrote procedures and manuals covering employment, benefits, wages and salaries, and training. Conducted contract negotiations with 12 unions, concerning service personnel in many categories.

Education
1970

Fordham University, New York.
DEGREE: B.S.   MAJOR SUBJECT: Personnel Administration

New York University (Graduate Division), New York
25 credits in Personnel, Wage & Salary and Welfare Administration

ALICE COOPERSMITH
12 James Place
Philadelphia, PA 19112
(215) 555-9280

EDITOR — REPORTER
PUBLIC RELATIONS MANAGER

Special skills, acquired during thirty years of newspaper and public relations work, include extensive reporting, writing and rewriting, editing and related activities in both spot news and feature writing, as well as project planning and execution of special programs and activities in public relations for a variety of both profit and nonprofit organizations. Such activities have included conceptual as well as operational responsibilities and heavy contact with both clients and media.

EXPERIENCE

January 1985-present: AMERICAN HEALTH FOUNDATION, Philadelphia, Pennsylvania
Assistant Public Relations Manager. Responsible for media placement including newspaper, magazine, television, radio. Duties include initiation and development of newsworthy projects. Heavy personal contacts with all major and most minor news outlets. Stories and personalities tied to newsworthy concepts are placed with news, feature, talk and special events shows on radio and TV as well as in all major newspaper and magazine outlets.

January 1962-September 1985: THE EVENING NEWS-BULLETIN, Trenton, New Jersey
General News Reporter and Writer. General assignment, rewrite, spot and feature writing for daily and Sunday editions as well as Sunday magazine supplement. In the course of 24 years with this leading metropolitan daily, covered or participated in the coverage of every major story in south New Jersey, as well as major stories out-of-state which were of special importance to the paper. Also worked on the rewrite desk and supplied stories to major news services and magazines on a special assignment basis.

Miscellaneous and freelance work — Have worked extensively as a news consultant for a number of both profit and nonprofit organizations. Have maintained an extremely close liaison with key governmental authorities on Federal, State, and local levels, as well as those in the judiciary and in the administrative and political agencies.

EDUCATION

RUTGERS UNIVERSITY-RUTGERS COLLEGE, New Jersey. Degree: **B.S. in Journalism**

CAROL KORWIN
4 Interstate Place
Atlanta, GA 64381
(404) 555-5270

**ADMINISTRATIVE ASSISTANT
EXECUTIVE SECRETARY**

EXPERIENCE:
1985-present

Peter Jones, Inc. — Insurance Brokers
400 William Street, Atlanta, Georgia

Administrative Assistant to the Vice-President. Duties include secretarial work, heavy client contact and general office details.

1977-1985

American Cosmetics Industries, Inc.
1227 Stenton Avenue, Atlanta, Georgia

Administrative Assistant to the Executive Vice-President and Director of Marketing. Duties included secretarial work, handling advertising traffic details, setting up, attending and supervising sales meeting held throughout the country. Maintenance of EDP records, hiring personnel, acting in close liaison with the company President and Chairman of the Board when the Executive Vice-President was not available.

1972-1975

Amporg Management Corporation — Management Consultants
69 Easton Road, Atlanta, Georgia

Secretary to the President. General administrative duties. Handled both office and personal business. Organized conferences. Arranged trade association meetings. Supervised stenographic and typing pool.

1967-1972

Hotel Georgian
Atlanta Georgia

Personal Secretary to the President. This position included coordinating the activities of the clerical staff in the front office and maintaining records of all subsidiary offices.

SKILLS:

- Shorthand — 150 words per minute
- Typing — 80 words per minute
- Knowledge of calculators and billing machines
- Familiar with Lotus 1-2-3

EDUCATION:

Georgia State University, Atlanta, Georgia — 2 years

Laramee Secretarial School, Atlanta, Georgia

JACK R. KELLER
1022 Langley Avenue
Warminster, PA 18974
(215) 555-5879

====================

SALES REPRESENTATIVE

EXPERIENCE:

June 1987
to Present

Fortune Sewing Machine Company
120 Texas Avenue, Ardmore, PA

Sales Representative. Currently selling high quality in-home use sewing machines to independent dealers. Have produced a 20% growth in sales in existing accounts, and have established new business in a high-turnover territory.

May 1987
May 1986

Ranier Company, Inc.
1475 Adams Street, Philadelphia, PA

Branch Salesman. Sold electric mixing machines to mass merchandisers, catalog stores, and independent retailers. Produced a sales growth of 50% in my territory.

October 1986
April 1983

General Appliance Corporation
1260 Willets Road, Philadelphia, PA

Territory Salesman. Sold 200 assorted small appliances to jobbers, mass merchandisers, and catalog houses plus independent retailers. In the Delaware Valley market, was a leader in new sales and maintained a steady increase in volume among established accounts.

EDUCATION:

Montgomery County Community College
King of Prussia, Pennsylvania
Associate Degree in Business

Beatrice Letterman
2694 Royer Street
Macon, GA 30247
(404) 555-5887

Objective:

To find long-term employment in the credit department of a company that offers a challenging and rewarding career with advancement opportunities and compensation.

Experience:

GEORGIA GAS COMPANY, Macon, Georgia — 1971-1993

1980-1993: *Credit Representative.* Responsible for control and maintenance of approximately 7000 accounts, collection of past-due invoices; resolving disputes; communicating with customers by telephone or correspondence. Decision-making responsibility for suspension of credit and approval of credit up to $1000 on established accounts. Recommend transfer of accounts to in-house collection unit or outside collection agency after all practical means of collection have been exhausted.

1978-1980: *Collection Representative.* Performed collection activities through use of telephone, computer, and word processing letters in the in-house collection unit.

1974-1978: *Customer Representative—Collections.* Serviced and maintained collection accounts through placement with outside agencies. Reviewed and granted suit authorization when requested and handled to conclusion all correspondence from agencies, courts, debtors, and attorneys.

1971-1974: *Accounting Clerk.* Maintained records on accounts, posted and balanced payment from customers, and typed daily reports. Entered data into computer terminal regarding customer credit limits and other pertinent information.

Education:

CENTRAL HIGH SCHOOL, Macon, Georgia — 1970
Commercial Course.

OTHER:

Business Correspondence Workshop
Telephone Seminar
Dictaphone Technique Seminar
Word Processing Course

References:

Available upon request

SALLY J. BROWN
2016 N. Nowell Street
Yonkers, NY 10709
(914) 555-4573 — days
(914) 555-4357 — evenings

CAREER OBJECTIVE   A responsible position utilizing my business experience and computer knowledge.

EDUCATION
1982-1983   **Fairchild Data Systems Institute,** Edison, N.J. Successfully completed a 500-hour course which covered structured programming, tables, searches, and indexing.

Languages: ANS COBOL, BAL, RPG II AND OS/VS JCL

1978-1982   **Long Island University,** Brooklyn, N.Y.
B.S. Mathematics

EMPLOYMENT HISTORY
1986-Present   **Health Services, Inc.** — 25 W. 45th St., New York, N.Y.

Medical Claims Manager — Supervise the Data Entry coding department. Implement methods, procedures affecting the claims coding area to improve department performance. Coordinate the systems and data entry department in the development from manual to an on-line processing department. Worked with the utilization review area to insure the proper handling and timely processing of medical claims. Familiar with CPT-4 and ICD-9 coding procedures.

1984-1986   **Midway General Hospital** — Brooklyn, N.Y.

Systems and Procedures Analyst — Coordinate Data Entry functions for patient billing operations. Recommend program and system modifications for automation of system. Troubleshoot problems. Assist in EDP auditing. Interface with user in department in solving problems regarding smooth workflow.

1982-1984   **Washington National Bank** — White Plains, N.Y.

Assistant to Credit Department Manager — Help prepare and coordinate the overlimit department for the Visa card center. Contact with other bank departments. Work with on-line terminal using CRT 3278 Module II.

MARVIN LANDERS

156 Sanders Drive   •   Teaneck, NJ 07042   •   (201) 555-2406

OBJECTIVE: Sales or marketing position with potential for unlimited growth and responsibilities

EDUCATION:
May 1985

Susquehanna University, Selinsgrove, PA
Degree: B.S.
Majors: Finance and Marketing
Minor: Economics
Computer Courses: Basic and Microcomputers

EXPERIENCE:
1987-Present

Arco Products Corporation, Secaucus, NJ
Sales Representative

Covered New Jersey and Eastern Pennsylvania territories for major manufacturer of household products. Contacted store buying offices of wholesalers, rack jobbers, and retail accounts.

- Opened Brite-Aid Drug Chain, New Jersey and Pennsylvania, for direct buying through regional distribution.
- Supervised all Brite-Aid direct buying drop shipment programs in both territories with volume of $500,000 annually.
- Participated in training programs for new sales representatives in territory.
- Opened new direct buying account with anticipated volume in excess of $100,000.
- Responsible for supermarket rack programs for Foodway, Keystone Superettes, and Fair Deal Supermarkets in territories.

1985-1986

Brighton Distributing Company, New York, NY
Sales Representative

- Covered Northern New Jersey and Rockland County, New York for all Farmspring Beverage products.
- Called on and sold to all supermarkets and grocery outlets in the territory.
- Worked with the Sales Manager in promoting cooperative advertising programs based on sales potentials for various retail chain outlets.
- Increased sales volume for territory by 15% during first four months of sales efforts.

1983-1985

Rowland Produce Company, Lawrenceville, NJ
Billing Clerk — Part-time

Fielding Photo Shop, Teaneck, NJ
Sales Clerk — Summer position

SYLVIA M. MORRISON
1423 Lewis Drive
Ardmore, PA 15906
(215) 555-6785

EXECUTIVE SECRETARY

SUMMARY

Over 14 years of secretarial experience with a major corporation in positions of increasing responsibility. Excellent secretarial and administrative skills plus the ability to work with corporate executives at all levels.

EXPERIENCE

WILLMOTT INDUSTRIAL CHEMICAL COMPANY, Willow Grove, PA

1987-1993 — **Executive Secretary.** Report to the Director of Personnel. Responsible for maintaining highly confidential employee records, preparing correspondence, maintaining absentee records and vacation schedules, handling domestic travel arrangements, monitoring incoming correspondence, and processing invoices.

- Set up a training program for typists on newly acquired word processing system.
- Helped organize work flow system to eliminate duplication and enable office staff to complete assignments on schedule.
- Interviewed and recommended hiring of secretarial and clerical staff.
- Assisted employees relocating to Cleveland facility with travel and relocation procedures and corporate plans and documents.

1981-1987 — **Administrative Assistant.** Report to Assistant Manager, Human Resources. Performed general secretarial duties, arranged meetings and appointments, maintained files and records. Directed secretarial work flow. Recorded staff meetings and typed reports for other departments.

1977-1981 — **Secretary-Stenographer.** Report to Director of Compensation and Benefits. Responsibilities include all secretarial duties in addition to preparing all correspondence.

1974-1977 — **Stenographer** — Report to Assistant Director of Marketing. Performed routine stenographic duties.

EDUCATION

1972-1974 — **Ambler Business College**, Ambler, PA

1966-1972 — **Willow Grove High School**, Willow Grove, PA
Commercial Courses

TRAINING COURSES AND SEMINARS
- Professional Secretary Seminar
- Building Team Effectiveness Program
- Introduction to Computers
- Wang Word Processor Course
- Basic Accounting Course

NANCY K. ARNOLD
1694 Clay Avenue
Bronx, NY 10463
(718) 555-4563

DATA PROCESSING PROGRAMMER PROGRAM ANALYST

HARDWARE: DEC, IBM, HONEYWELL
LANGUAGES: FORTRAN, IV, F77, COBOL
DATABASES: HISAM, OLIVER, NOMAD

EDUCATION:

NEW YORK UNIVERSITY, New York, N.Y.
B.S. Computer Science

EXPERIENCE:

July 1985–
May 1993

NATIONAL BANK & TRUST CO.
New York, N.Y.

Programmer Analyst
Responsible for design, analysis, and code
enhancements for sub-system of a leading cash
management operation.

Analyze, design, and code various utility
programs to provide product management and
service to customer accounts and credit and
debit and balance data.

Coding and testing of credit/debit and balance
modules of cash management system rewrite.
Programs were written in FORTRAN IV AND 77
utilizing extraction data manipulation (HISAM).

June 1983–
July 1985

NATIONAL DATA SYSTEMS, INC.
New York, N.Y.

Technical Representative
Responsibilities involved design, coding,
testing, and documenting customized client
software application packages. Preparing
estimates of development time and production
costs, interfacing with clients during
requirement analysis, and installation.

Created standard software demonstrations.
Increased client revenues by defining sales
opportunities.

Taught courses for database package, timesharing, and practical terminal experience.

ROBERT FRAWLEY
RD # 6 BOX 432
LAWRENCE, KS 66043
(913) 555-4578

MASTER MACHINIST
MECHANICAL CRAFTSMAN

Fifteen years experience in construction, maintenance, and field service of automated machinery. Specialized in electronically controlled hydraulic, pneumatic, and vacuum systems, including the maintenance of system components such as pumps, compressors, valves, etc. Experienced in machining and welding.

WORK EXPERIENCE

1983-1993	MIDWEST RESEARCH & DEVELOPMENT CO., Topeka, KS	
	Senior Craftsman — Mechanical	**1985-1993**
	Craftsman I	**1984-1985**
	Craftsman II	**1983-1984**

- Repaired and serviced a wide variety of mechanical devices and equipment without supervision.
- Skills include testing equipment, troubleshooting, fabricating and recondition of parts, on-site removal and installation of equipment and interpretation of drawings.
- Operation of variety of tools, lifting devices, cleaning machinery, and machine shop equipment.
- Handling of mechanical emergencies, maintenance, and general operation of the fuel distribution facility, and record keeping.
- Supervision of shift in absence of foreman.

1978-1983   GILMAN-LEWIS CORPORATION, Lawrence, KS
Master Assembler

- Supervised construction of machinery for major automated foundry equipment company.

1977-1978   PETCO CORPORATION, Kansas City, KS
Mechanic — Industrial equipment

1973-1976   UNITED STATES AIR FORCE
Aircraft Mechanic

EDUCATION

1983	**ICS Machining Course**
1973	Diploma from **US Air Force Aircraft Pneudraulics School**
1972	Diploma from **Technical Institute**, Lawrence, KS
1971	Graduate of **Central High School**, Kansas City, KS

MICHAEL RICHMAN

2122 S. Beechwood Drive   •   Los Angeles, CA 90068   •   (213) 555-6823

FINANCIAL SYSTEMS ANALYST/PROGRAMMER

Seasoned MIS/Research professional with background in the banking and securities industries. Possess strong communications, analytical, and management skills. Fully experienced in DP/MIS.

CAREER HISTORY

American Bank & Trust Company   **1990-Present**
200 Warnock Blvd.
Burbank, CA 91532
SENIOR PROGRAM ANALYST

- Develop and implement systems and procedures for equities department.
- Organize an efficient systems operation that responds quickly to management and user needs.
- Insure easy access to information resulting in faster problem-solving techniques.
- Enable observations to be made regarding the system's impact on customer satisfaction.
- Write procedures manuals to train computer operators.
- Determine the feasibility of new equipment to improve efficiency and advise management.

Southwest Fidelity Trust Company   **1987-1990**
461 Broad Street
Los Angeles, CA 90063
PROGRAMMER

Provided continuous computer support for this multi-financial banking firm, and was directly responsible for the following:

- Individual bank reports to enable management to gauge branch office performance.
- Time and motion studies to improve customer transaction time.
- Development of system specifications for automatic transfer of data, thereby effecting substantial annual savings.
- Planning and implementation of correspondence tracking system to improve flow of information between individual bank branches and customers.
- Preparation and implementation of a spreadsheet program to determine work load and staffing requirements.

Continued...

EDUCATION

Arizona State University   **1981-1985**
B.S. COMPUTER SCIENCE

Stanford University   **1985-1987**
MS INFORMATION SYSTEMS

MISCELLANEOUS

- Completed IBM program in Financial Programming

- Member of American Banking Association

- Member of Association of Computer Programmers

REFERENCES AVAILABLE UPON REQUEST

MARCIA ALLEN
231 Franklin Street
Indianapolis, IN 46204
(317) 555-4765

WORD PROCESSOR

EDUCATION
1980 — **Franklin Business Schools**

1981 — **Indianapolis Data Processing Institute**

EXPERIENCE
January 1989 to December 1993
Indiana Trust Company, Indianapolis, IN

Word Processor. Worked on correspondence, financial statements, charts, credit reports, and inter-office communications.

February 1987 to November 1989
National Steel Works, Indianapolis, IN

Secretary to Purchasing Manager. General secretarial duties. Correspondence, reports, presentations, and memos using WordStar program.

April 1982 to January 1987
Indiana Motor Vehicles Bureau, Indianapolis, IN

Data Entry Clerk. Promoted after one year to senior operator responsible for training of new data entry clerks and scheduling work flow.

October 1980 to April 1982
Midtown Temps, Inc., Indianapolis, IN

Temporary Worker. Worked through temporary placement agency. Assignments included a variety of firms and positions, including clerical, secretarial and word processing.

SOFTWARE AND OFFICE SKILLS
• WordStar 5.5
• WordPerfect 5.1
• MultiMate
• PageMaker
• Microsoft Word
• Lotus 1-2-3
• Typing: 85 WPM
• Steno: 110 WPM

Ann O' Sullivan
253 59th Avenue
Kansas City, MO 65043
(816) 555-3845

Objective: To obtain a challenging position where I can effectively utilize my training and experience in the field of Social Work.

Summary: Experience in social work includes both private and public agencies. Can offer intelligence, curiosity, analytical ability, and the capability to work independently. Possess excellent oral and written communications skills.

Employment:
January 1980 to
December 1993

CHILDREN'S AID SOCIETY, Topeka, Kansas

Adoption Counselor. While employed with this major childrens' adoption service, duties included:

- Directing and processing client intake program.
- Interviewing and processing clients.
- Providing therapeutic counseling services to prospective clients.
- Preparing and documenting investigative reports for the county courts.
- Supervising a staff of administrative clerical aides.

November 1977 to
January 1980

KANSAS CITY DEPARTMENT OF SOCIAL SERVICES, Kansas City, Missouri

Social Worker. As a staff member of this large city social service agency, was responsible for:

- Diagnostic and therapeutic services to families experiencing stress or disruption.
- Marital and family counseling, both on a preventive and crises-intervention basis.

Achievements: Received promotions in all employment situations. Attained senior level position with corresponding authority and responsibility.

Successfully met defined goals within allotted time limits.

Established effective assessment approach in interviewing clients.

Developed leadership skills through attendance at seminars and workshops related to my occupation.

Achieved interpersonal skills to work effectively in a multi-racial environment.

Education:
1977
1975

KANSAS STATE UNIVERSITY, Manhattan, Kansas
Master of Social Work
BA in English Literature

NANCY PETAIN
4814 North Eighth Street
Philadelphia, PA 19153
(215) 555-1212

DENTAL HYGIENIST

EDUCATION:

1989   **School of Dental Hygiene**
                        Temple University, Philadelphia, PA
                        Certificate of graduation

1985   **Central High School,** Philadelphia, PA
                        Diploma — General Course

EMPLOYMENT:

8/91   **Jerome Baron, D.D.S. [Orthodontist]**
 to   1475 Roosevelt Boulevard
12/93   Philadelphia, PA 19163
                        HYGIENIST

- Recorded patients' medical histories
- Took x-rays and developed film
- Performed oral prophylaxis
- Took and recorded blood pressure
- Did cavity and oral cancer surveys
- Gave fluoride treatment
- Assisted in post-operative procedures
- Removed plaque
- Instructed patients on oral hygiene

10/89   **Richard Tennant, D.D.S. [General Practice]**
 to   42 Park Drive
7/91   Willow Grove, PA 19254
                        DENTAL ASSISTANT & HYGIENIST

- Prepared patients for dental examination
- Developed x-rays
- Took cavity surveys
- Charted patients' mouths
- Sterilized instruments
- Prepared insurance forms for billing
- Confirmed appointments

PERSONAL: Member of the American Dental Hygiene Society
                        Licensed by Commonwealth of Pennsylvania

Elaine Klein, R.N.
460 Balfour Avenue
Teaneck, N.J. 07320
(201) 555-6094

Objective	To obtain a challenging position in a community-based agency, health clinic or medical facility which rewards creativity for quality health care.

Education
1980

State University at Stony Brook, New York
Bachelor of Science in Nursing

Experience
Sept. 1990-
Present

Northeast Medical Group, Staten Island, New York
UTILIZATION REVIEW SPECIALIST

• Medicare on-site review activities
• Quality assurance of patient care
• Pre-admission patient screening
• DRG validation
• Insurance carrier review analyst
• Billing audits

Aug. 1981-
Aug. 1990

Franklin Memorial Medical Center, Teaneck, New Jersey
CHARGE NURSE — RESPIRATORY I.C.U.

• Unit management
• Delegation of nurses' assignments
• Coordination of activities and schedules
  of intensive care unit

STAFF R.N. — RESPIRATORY I.C.U.

• Patient assessment
• Documentation of patient care
• Assist doctors with emergency procedures

STAFF R.N. — SURGERY UNIT

• Post-surgical patient care
• Patient instructions and referrals to out-patient
  clinic, and community services

Personal

N.Y. State Board for Nursing Lic #354-98
N.J. State Board for Nursing Lic # NR 53924
Member: *American Nurses Association*
        Society of Health Care Professionals

LORRAINE BUTLER
625 East 3rd Street
Brooklyn, NY 11223
(718) 555-7463

PARALEGAL

OBJECTIVE:
　　To join a law firm or a corporate legal department where I can use my training and experience as a Paralegal.

EDUCATION:
Metropolitan Business School, New York, NY — 1989 to 1990
　　Paralegal Studies Program. Awarded Certificate of Distinction in Paralegal studies.
　　Intensive, in-depth program that included:
- office management
- legal research
- estate administration
- procedures for the probate of wills
- legal terminology

James Madison High School, New York, NY — 1985 to 1989
　　Commercial Courses. Subjects included:
- commercial law
- bookkeeping
- basic word processing
- typing
- shorthand

WORK EXPERIENCE:
Mid-Atlantic Insurance Co., Inc., 1515 Broadway, New York, NY — 1991 to Present
　　Legal Secretary to House Counsel. Responsibilities include:
- taking dictation
- typing correspondence and legal documents
- maintaining appointment calendar
- acting as general administrative assistant

Office of the District Attorney, New York State Supreme Court Building, Brooklyn, NY — 1989 to 1991
　　General Clerk. Responsibilities included:
- collating of legal papers
- typing of documents
- correspondence and telephone
  contact with other legal agencies

STEVEN KAGLE

6290 Essex Street   Boston, MA 02284   (617) 555-3987

MARKETING/SALES ADMINISTRATOR

OBJECTIVE: To obtain a position with a progressive firm where I can utilize my organizational, administrative and managerial skills to make a real contribution to its growth and profitability.

EXPERIENCE:

July 1986-
Sept. 1993

McCartney Medical Services, Inc.
4935 Radcliffe Street, Brockton, MA 02121
ASSISTANT SALES MANAGER

Responsibilities:
•Supervised and directed the activities and performance of the company's sales staff.
•Recruited, interviewed and hired all sales personnel.
•Developed and promoted new areas of business to increase overall sales volume.
•Detail physicians, nursing homes, social workers, physical therapists and other
 professionals in the medical field.
•Introduced and promoted the use of new medical products to surgeons, nurses
 and hospital medical personnel.
•In-service hospital assistance with new products.
•Oversaw the operation of company store outlets in the absence of store managers.

July 1982-
June 1986

Lincoln Carpet Company
2792 Emerald Street, Brockton, MA 02016
SALES REPRESENTATIVE

Responsibilities:
•Estimated costs on carpet, furniture and drapery cleaning.
•Appraised fire damage, carpet removal and reinstallation services.
•Initiated contract cleaning arrangements.

1978-
1981

U.S. Army
SERGEANT-PROCUREMENT

1976-
1978

Macy's Department Store
Brockton, MA 02017
ASSISTANT DEPARTMENT MANAGER

•Entered in management training program
•Promoted to salesman
•Advanced to assistant manager

PERSONAL: Willing to travel or relocate
Completed course in medical products

The Functional Resume

The chronological resume described in the preceding section is the most commonly used. It enables the reader to review your background in an orderly time sequence.

There are circumstances, however, under which the chronological resume may prove harmful—if your work background is spotty, for instance. If you have held several positions within a relatively short period of time, the chronological resume will give the impression of job instability. This may have been due to circumstances beyond your control, such as mergers, bankruptcies, or relocation. Or, you may have moved frequently before you found the right spot.

Unfortunately, many personnel people tend to make a quick judgment when they see a long list of jobs held within a short period of time, without making an attempt to discover why. If you recall, in Chapter 1, I said that resume screening is primarily a process of elimination. Those applicants eliminated first are those with frequent job changes.

The functional resume described in this chapter does not change your work record. It presents it in a different form so that the reader will be more interested in what you did than in how long you did it.

Some Basic Information

If you study the sample resumes on pages 63-74, you will see that the basic information is the same, but it is arranged in such a way that the reader is drawn to a description of your duties and accomplishments and not the number of jobs you have held. Of course, you cannot omit the names of your employers but this is reserved for last and by the time the reader has reached it, he has, hopefully, been convinced of your competence.

Let's review the topics that should appear in all resumes:

(1) Identification
(2) Job Objective
(3) Experience
(4) Education
(5) Miscellaneous Information

In this functional resume these headings are rearranged and another category is added—the summary. This will appear directly under your job objective and will take up a large part of your resume, the entire first page, if necessary.

For example, here is a good summary taken from a functional resume written by a financial analyst and writer:

"Twelve years' experience with leading brokerage firms as security analyst and portfolio manager, with responsibility for analysis of financial data and determination of proper securities for inclusion in customers' portfolios.

PORTFOLIO MANAGER: Exercised discretionary authority for individual investment accounts. Maintained close liaison with internal research department and investment banking specialists, resulting in substantial appreciation of the value of supervised accounts.

SECURITY ANALYST: Initiated research programs and created industry studies on corporation developments and general financial publications. Did extensive field work, contacting management in corporate and institutional organizations.

COMMUNICATIONS: Wrote lengthy in-depth reports, directed to management, relating to the financial condition and potential for growth of individual corporations and on an industry-wide basis."

The reader of this resume is told immediately, and in detail, just what the applicant has done, before he gets into the company identification, education, age, or any other aspect of the background. Any weaknesses in subsequent portions will probably be offset by the summary.

Here is another summary taken from the resume of an applicant who, because of a merger, relocation, and bankruptcy, held four jobs in nine years. Had he used the chronological form, listing his jobs first, he might have given the impression of being a job hopper which would have hampered his chances for an interview. The summary indicates a strong background and professional competence that cannot be overlooked.

"Nine years of editorial and public relations experience, after receiving a journalism degree from Pennsylvania State University. This experience included such highlights as:

—Technical editor and local-office public relations manager for a consulting firm in the urban planning field. Wrote reports, proposals, and articles while serving national clients in the industry.
—Public relations aide for the trade association of the urban mass transportation industry. Supervised the publication of promotional material for members.
—Designed and created a company magazine for a major transportation company under the direction of the public relations director. Also wrote press releases and feature articles for trade and consumer media.
—Associate editor for a leading industrial trade magazine; writing articles and general news, and editing twice-a-month magazine for the machine tool industry, including all phases of production, planning, makeup, and layout. Also wrote for the new products section and other business and financial departments. In connection with this position I also wrote a special monthly newsletter on general business and financial developments in the industry and trends and other items of interest to machine tool manufacturers and users."

List Your Employers

The next heading in your functional resume, directly under your summary, should be titled "Experience." Under this heading, list the positions you held starting with the last. Include only your title, the dates of your employment, and the company name and address. It is not necessary to repeat your duties and accomplishments with each company, as you have already covered this in your initial summary.

Here is how a typical experience section will look in this functional resume:

October, 1985 to October, 1991	Editor Hawking, Waring, Johnson & Kelly, Inc. 2400 Roosevelt Blvd. Philadelphia, Pa. 19154
September, 1981 to August, 1985	Public Relations Assistant American Public Transportation Assn. 3234 Main Street Jenkintown, Pa. 19268

June, 1979 to August, 1981	Assistant Public Relations Manager Intercity Transportation Company 815 Chestnut Street Philadelphia, Pa 19144
February, 1976 to April, 1979	Associate Editor *Industrial World* Lawrence Publishing Company 225 Lamston Street Pittsburg, Pa

Glancing at this sequence, the prospective employer can readily follow the applicant's career from his first job to his last. It is not necessary to list your duties although you may repeat the highlights if you wish.

Directly after your experience, list your education and miscellaneous information in the same manner as you would in the chronological form.

Sample Resumes — Functional Form

JANICE GALLAGER
1261 Randolph Street
Saddle River, N.J. 07324
(201) 555-6935

PROFESSION:	Programmer
EXPERIENCE:	Two years' diversified programming experience

HARDWARE:
- 370/155
- Prime 550

SOFTWARE:
- OS/JCL under MVS
- COBOL and RPGII
- BASIC and PL1
- ASSEMBLER

- Programs written utilizing STRUCTURED PROGRAMMING

- Extensive experience with EBDIC MACHINE LANGUAGE, DEBUGGING and SOURCE CODE DEBUGGING

APPLICATIONS:
- Accounts payable
- Accounts receivable
- Inventory
- Sales analysis and forecasting

EMPLOYMENT:
1988 to
present

Centrifax Management Resources, Inc.
149 W. 18th Street
Little Falls, N.J.

Position: **Programmer**

EDUCATION:
1987

New York University
New York, N.Y.

Degree: **B.S. Computer Science**

Ralph Dickson
123 S. 45th Street
Philadelphia, PA 19104
(215) 555-3222

ACCOUNTING/FINANCIAL MANAGEMENT

EXTENSIVE BACKGROUND IN ALL PHASES OF ACCOUNTING, SYSTEMS AND FINANCIAL ANALYSIS

General Accounting
Supervised and prepared all entries in books of original entry and subsidiary ledgers. Prepared tax returns on federal, state and city levels.

Financial Reports
Prepared monthly and annual financial reports, along with comparative analysis of similar periods.

Auditing
Performed and supervised detailed audits of balance sheet and income statement accounts.

Cost Accounting
Worked closely with many clients in setting up cost systems for present plus future production plans.

Systems
Helped streamline accounting procedures of clients by use of modern systems (one-write systems, IBM inventory controls).

Experience
Nov.1976-
Present

MADISON INDUSTRIES, INC. (manufacturing)
480 Lexington Avenue
Philadelphia, PA 14563

Assistant Controller — Financial responsibility and control of multiplant division with sales volume in excess of $14 million annually.

Nov. 1966-
Nov. 1976

LARRABEE MANUFACTURING CO.
832 Midland Street
Brooklyn, NY 11245

Accountant — Responsibilities included direct participation in complete accounting function. Developed and installed overhead allocation system used in cost accounting.

Education
Jan. 1966

CITY COLLEGE OF NEW YORK
BBA in Accounting

Sylvia Friedman
95 Girard Avenue
Camden, N.J. 07820
(609) 555-3767

Objective:

A position in computer sales with a company that offers an opportunity for ultimate management responsibility.

Sales Experience:

- Sales of CAD/CAM Software to companies in Pennsylvania, New Jersey, and New York.

- Attained 125% of my quota in orders received in assigned territory.

- Turnkey mini-computer sales in retail, wholesale, manufacturing, and service industries.

- Opened new accounts which brought in over $90,000 over a period of one year.

- Sold timesharing and remote batch services to companies of all sizes in the area of Delaware County, PA.

- Developed new business and increased sales to established accounts.

Technical Experience:

- Knowledge of COBOL, BASIC, and FORTRAN for the IBM 370/155.

- Excellent knowledge of NUMERICAL CONTROL.

- Familiar with flow diagrams for chemical plant processes.

- Proficient in computer applications for accounts receivables, accounts payables, and inventory systems.

Employment:
1988-1993

RTW Industries
260 W. Moreland Street, Princeton, NJ
Position: Computer Sales

1987-1988

Arlington Foster Co., Inc.
195 Main Street, Warminster, PA
Position: Assistant to Sales Manager

1985-1987

Amereast Construction Corporation
14 Lawrence Street, Chester, PA
Position: Administrative Assistant

Education:
1981-1985

Pennsylvania State University, University Park, PA
Degree: BA in English

Personal:

Available for travel and/or relocation
References on request

CHARLES LEE

141 Clay Street • San Francisco, CA 94117 • (415) 555-2453

COMPUTER OPERATOR

OBJECTIVE: Computer Operator

TECHNICAL KNOWLEDGE:

Hardware:	3033, 370/168
	360/30, 3705
	3800, 3211
Software:	OS/VSI, MVS/JES II
	VM, DOS, HASP
	CICS, JCL

SUMMARY OF EXPERIENCE:

Five years experience on large-scale 370 systems, mainly in production environment with JCL.

Excellent knowledge in the concept of operating systems and hardware utilization in a service bureau environment.

Experienced in running a computer room and scheduling operations.

Testing, batching real-time and production background including R.J.E. and Cathode-Ray Tube terminals.

WORK EXPERIENCE:

1984-Present

Central California Bank & Trust Co.
San Francisco, California
Computer Room Supervisor — Responsible for scheduling and work flow.

1982-1984

Western Mutual Insurance Co.
San Francisco, California
Computer Operator — Worked on 370 operating systems.

1980-1982

Hayward Service Bureau
San Francisco, California
Computer Operator and Production Coordinator — Maintained production schedules. Checked equipment capabilities and performed customer relations duties.

EDUCATION:

1980

Technical Community College, San Francisco, CA
Computer Science

1978

Berkeley High School, Berkeley, CA

ROBERT MICHAELS
1475 Grand Concourse
Bronx, N.Y. 10467
(718) 555-9857

OBJECTIVE

A challenging and rewarding position utilizing my broad skills and experience in Data Processing.

Technical Capabilities
Hardware: IBM 4331, 370/135, 370/125, 360/30, Datapoint 6700

Software: COBOL, BAL, DATABUS, DOS/VSE, VSAM, ICCF, ISAM, POWER/VS

EDUCATION

Long Island University
Brooklyn, New York
B.S. Mathematics

North American Computer Institute
New York, New York

EXPERIENCE

- Analysis, design, programming, and user training of all company systems, including accounts receivable, accounts payable, sales analysis and forecasting, inventory control, production scheduling, and payroll
- Conversions from IBM 360 and 370 computers to IBM 4330 systems
- Evaluation and procurement of data entry equipment, main frame computers, software, and other major equipment
- Originated concepts and wrote software programs in COBOL, BAL, and DATABUS

EMPLOYMENT HISTORY

1984-Present

Larabee Publishing Co.
315 E. 52nd Street, New York, N.Y.
Assistant Data Processing Manager

1981-1983

Freeport Typographic Co.
230 W. Portland Street, Ft. Lee, N.J.
Programming Analyst

1978-1981

National Insurance Corp.
23 Wall Street, New York, N.Y.
Systems and Programming Analyst

1975-1978

TRS Systems, Inc.
630 Fifth Avenue, New York, N.Y.
Programmer

MISCELLANEOUS

Member: *National Programmers Society*
Administrative Management Association
Association of Electronic Data Processing Managers

MARY B. REYNOLDS
966 Rosewood Avenue
Los Angeles, CA 95616
(916) 555-9104

MEDICAL RECORDS ADMINISTRATOR

POSITION OBJECTIVE: A challenging position in the medical information or medical records field where extensive experience and education may be utilized.

SUMMARY OF QUALIFICATIONS:

Diversified practical experience in the following disciplines:
- Research compilation of scientific/medical data
- Abstracting and indexing medical and scientific documents
- Maintaining and updating storage and retrieval systems
- Clinical laboratory techniques
- Quality control methods and procedures

Demonstrated ability to accept increasing responsibility.

Capable of initiating and implementing major decisions.

Leadership qualities combined with ability to pioneer in new techniques and projects.

Ability to communicate effectively at all levels.

Experienced in applying principles of good management.

EMPLOYMENT RECORD:
October 1987-1993

ASSISTANT MEDICAL LIBRARIAN
Langston Pharmaceutical Corp.
480 Summer Street, Los Angeles, CA

Responsibilities include:
- Abstracting and indexing articles from medical journals.
- Searching and compiling literature for various company divisions, such as sales, legal, and marketing.
- Setting up and maintaining proper storage and retrieval systems.
- Cross-referencing abstract cards according to subject heading and sub-heading.
- Retrieving all published data required for submission to the F.D.A.

Continued...

Jan. 1981-Sept. 1987   CHIEF TECHNICIAN
                            Davis County Hospital
                            Sacramento, California

                            Responsible for the organization of a functional clinical
                            laboratory in setting up and standardizing clinical procedures
                            and practices; procurement of supplies and equipment for
                            testing and analysis of laboratory specimens.

Dec. 1979-Dec. 1981   CLINICAL TECHNICIAN
                            Lathrobe General Hospital
                            Davis, California

                            Performed routine clinical testing and analysis of specimens
                            submitted from various departments of the hospital. Assisted
                            chief laboratory technician in all administrative functions of
                            the department. Collected data and made statistical analysis
                            of all tests that funnelled through the laboratory. Submitted
                            data to department heads when requested.

**SUMMER AND PART-
TIME EMPLOYMENT:**
April 1977-Sept. 1979   LABORATORY INTERN
                            Memorial Hospital
                            San Francisco, California

                            While attending college, participated in laboratory
                            methodology and principles. Primary function was
                            private testing for director of laboratory.

EDUCATION:
1975-1979   **University of San Francisco**
                            San Francisco, California
                            B.S. BIOLOGY

1974   **Harrington Community College**
                            San Francisco, California
                            MEDICAL LABORATORY TECHNOLOGY

PERSONAL DATA: **License:** American Medical Technologist Association

ALBERT BLAINE

405 Severn Street • Fresno, CA 94102 • (209) 555-8592

OBJECTIVE: Promotion Manager

Sales Promotion — Devised and supervised sales promotion projects for large business firms and manufacturers in the electronics field. Originated newspaper, radio, and television advertising and coordinated sales promotion with public relations and sales management. Analyzed market potentials and developed new techniques to increase sales effectiveness and reduce sales costs. Developed sales training manuals.

As sales executive and promotion consultant, handled a variety of accounts. Was successful in raising the volume of sales in many of these firms 25 percent within the first year.

Sales Management — Hired and supervised sales staff on a local, area, and national basis. Established branch offices throughout the United States and developed uniform systems of processing orders and sales records. Promoted new products as well as improved sales of old ones. Develped sales training program. Developed a catalog system involving inventory control to facilitate stock movement.

Market Research — Devised and supervised market research projects to determine sales potentials, as well as need for advertising. Wrote detailed reports and recommendations describing each step in distribution, areas for development, and plans for sales improvement.

Sales — Retail and wholesale. Direct sales to consumer, jobber, and manufacturer. Handled hard goods, metals, and electrical appliances.

Order Clerk — Received, processed, and expedited orders. Set up order control system which was adopted for all branches.

EXPERIENCE:
1983-1993   **Sales Promotion Manager**
R.C. Loser Sales Corporation
1826 Harmes Avenue, San Francisco, CA

1977-1983   **Salesman**
Leonard Forrest Industrial Corp.
1625 West 2nd Street, Oakland, CA

1972-1977   **Sales Administrator**
Fanning Corporation
1325 Geary Street, San Francisco, CA

EDUCATION:
1980   **University of California**
Degree: B.S.   *Major:* Business Administration

REFERENCES: Available upon request

Mervin Stohl
427 Radcliffe Drive
Arlington, VA 39724
(302) 555-7648

Administrative Manager:

Directed administrative activities in large corporations. Skilled in office management, organization, work flow and measurement, systems and procedures, forms control, and personnel. Effected substantial savings through operational reviews and subsequent improvements. Knowledge of EDP.

Summary:

- Managed administrative activities in a department of 125 professionals and support staff of 50.
- Conducted operational reviews and studies of the activities and organization structure of client companies, resulting in a high percentage of acceptance on subsequent recommendations. Gained confidence of all levels of management.
- Analyzed and coordinated work flows, designed new and improved administrative, clerical, and mechanized systems, reduced staffing through work measurement techniques. Achieved payroll saving of 22%.
- Developed and improved purchasing, shipping, payroll, and billing procedures. Wrote procedure manuals and systems.
- Initiated study of clerical operations in purchasing department and attained a 24% reduction in department budget without decrease in efficiency.
- Installed forms control program that produced significant savings in cost of printing and operations.
- Assisted in the administration of a company's 12 branches. Introduced cost saving techniques that reduced overhead by 12%.

Company Affiliations:

1978-Present	**Stewart, Orins and Mayberry, Inc.** 365 18th Street, S.W., Washington, D.C. *Administrative Manager*
1974-1977	**Mentor Associates, Inc.** 1856 South Main Street, Baltimore, M.D. *Consultant*
1972-1974	**International Electric Corporation** Riverview Road, Baltimore, M.D. *Systems Analyst*
1970-1972	**Monograph Pictures Corporation** 73 West Madison Avenue, New York, N.Y. *Assistant Systems Manager*
1969-1970	**Eastern-American Life Insurance Co.** 576 Fifth Avenue, New York, N.Y. *Accountant*

Education:

New York University — *MBA, BS*

MARY AIELLO
91 Tabor Road
Los Angeles, CA 90065
(213) 555-6847

HEALTH ADMINISTRATOR — EPIDEMIOLOGIST IN DISEASE CONTROL

STRENGTHS
- Conduct investigative policies for disease control.
- Knowledge of public health administration.
- Ability to identify problems and implement effective solutions.
- Capable of dealing with crisis contingencies.
- Disciplined and well organized in work habits with ability to function smoothly in pressure situations.
- Skilled in motivating and interacting with co-workers.

ACHIEVEMENTS
- Intensive experience in Public Health Administration gained while associated with Dr. Frank Stenson, State Epidemiologist, California State Department of Health.
- Investigated outbreak of German measles and initiated epidemic control procedures.
- Researched and wrote paper on the Epidemiology of Asian Flu, published in the National Council of Health Bulletin.
- Adjudicator in the examination and determination of surgical and laboratory claims for the Providence Insurance Company.

EXPERIENCE

July 1986 to May 1993
Position: *Medical Technologist*

Los Angeles County Community Blood Bank
Los Angeles, California

May 1985 to May 1986
Position: *Epidemiologist*

California State Department of Health
Los Angeles, California

September 1982 to April 1985
Position: *Claims Adjudicator*

Providence Insurance Company
Beverly Hills, California

EDUCATION
University of California, Davis
MA Public Health — June 1980

PROFESSIONAL AFFILIATIONS
California Public Health Association
Society for Epidemiological Research

PHILLIP CANTOR
1642 Clay Street
San Francisco, CA 94119
(415) 555-3487

ENGINEERING/TECHNICAL WRITER

EDUCATION:

1978   **University of California, Davis — BSEE**

1974   **Western Technical College — AAS**

MANAGEMENT SKILLS:

As managing editor, supervised a staff of four editors. Initiated special editorial projects such as seminars on technical writing, a style book for authors, and the organization of a special "task force" to solve critical problems on all aspects of the publication.

WRITING:

Wrote technical articles for several national professional journals. Free-lanced stories covering all aspects of electronics and computers. Adept at interpreting technical jargon into readable English.

COMPUTER HARDWARE DESIGN:

As a project engineer for a large corporation, developed digital test equipment for a research and development project. Also designed and debugged computers and software.

SOFTWARE ENGINEER:

Created data base programs (dBASE III) for a major book and magazine publisher, and produced interactive software.

EMPLOYMENT HISTORY:

1987 to
Present

MANAGING EDITOR
Computer Age
460 Avery Way
Sacramento, CA 95801

1984 to
1987

TECHNICAL WRITER
Freelance

1979 to
1984

PROJECT ENGINEER
Entech Publishing
2640 N. 17th St.
San Jose, CA 95108

Carolyn King
125 Broad Street
Cleveland, Ohio 44102
(216) 555-4316

Objective
A position in retail merchandising or buying

Skills and Accomplishments
ORGANIZATION:
- Projected future sales based on the analysis of past sales history.
- Monitored performance of stores based on their individual income figures.
- Compared buyers' budgets to actual performance, and set future budgets and sales plans.
- Kept records of sales to stock ratio for all stores.

COMMUNICATIONS:
- Created and implemented a system for tracking sales, and designed applicable forms.
- Communicated with vendors by computer, telephone and in person.
- Maintained daily communication between store managers, buyers and warehouse supervisor.
- Wrote weekly bulletin announcing merchandising promotion campaigns for all stores.
- Coordinated with advertising department in preparing ads for local newspapers.

Employment History
1989-1993   MERCHANDISE PLANNER
              Fashion Plus, Cleveland

1987-1989   CONTROL BUYER
              StyleWear Ltd., Cleveland

1986-1987   MERCHANDISE PLANNER
              Leading Lady, Cleveland

Education
1983-1985   AAS DEGREE
              The Fashion Institute

1979-1983   DIPLOMA
              High School of Commerce

Resumes for Beginners

If you are a beginner looking for your first job, preparing a good resume can be more difficult than if you are an experienced job hunter. Since you have little or no experience there really is not much you can include, other than your name, address, phone number, and education. But even with that meager information you can compose a resume that would present your limited background in an informative way.

Start with your objective. As a trainee you may not know precisely what field you want to enter, so you may have to be a little vague about your objective. But this also will give you a wider choice of firms to contact.

One good job objective is always "Management Trainee." This does not restrict you to any particular field, but it does indicate that you are seeking a start in a position which will eventually lead to management.

If, however, you do have a definite goal, then indicate it as follows: Advertising Trainee—Junior Accountant—Personnel Assistant—Engineering Aide, etc.

Sell Your Education

Next, under your objective, state your education. This will be the main thrust of your resume since it is the only thing you have to sell. If you are a college graduate, there is no need to list your high school unless it was a technical or trade school. Begin by writing the inclusive dates of your college attendance, followed by the name of the college or university and the address. Following that, list your degree and your major field of study. It is not necessary to copy your official transcript on to your resume or list every subject taken. Your proficiency in physical training, Greek mythology, or some of the more exotic electives such as macrame, yoga, gourmet cooking, and belly dancing will not add one iota of value to your resume. Sports and hobbies fall into the same category. Company personnel managers are not really interested in your competence in surfing, tennis, chess, swimming or ping-pong. An interest in antiques, bridge, Siamese cats, or Charlie Chaplin films is very nice, but it is of doubtful value to the reader of your resume.

It is important, however, to list those subjects which have relevance to the career you are seeking. Be selective in choosing those subjects which will make your education more attractive. See the samples resumes for beginners on pages 77-79 for examples.

It is not necessary to list grade averages or class standing on your resume. Leave that for the interview, and don't volunteer it unless you are near the top of your class. However, if you won any honors, or made the Dean's List, or were awarded special citations or prizes, do put it in your resume.

Supplementary Schooling

Do not forget to list evening schools, home extension courses, trade association or professional seminars, and military service courses, if they are applicable. Every little bit helps. Did you belong to a professional fraternity or sorority? List it. Were you on the staff of any of your school publications? Did you do any teaching while you were at college? Say so. List all education-connected activities in which you participated. Each of these things will add to your image.

As a recent college graduate, your experience will, of course, be negligible. However, be sure to list formal internships or work study arrangements. These are considered valuable experience. Also show any experience you have, even if it consists of summer jobs or part-time employment. However menial, the fact that you have held some sort of a job will be a plus.

If you served in the Armed Forces, give the inclusive dates and the branch of service. If you were a commissioned officer, state your highest rank.

The last item on your resume should be about your references. A statement such as "references available upon request" will usually suffice on your resume. References, which generally include a professor or teacher plus one or two professional acquaintances, should be held for the interview.

Sample Resumes for Beginners

LEONORE M. ROOD
129 Radial Avenue
Bronxville, NY 10705
(914) 555-3217

MARKETING TRAINEE

OBJECTIVE:
Seeking entry-level position with a firm offering on-the-job training with an opportunity for advancement in the fields of marketing, research or advertising promotion.

EDUCATION:
February 1993

Columbia University, New York, New York
Degree: B.S. Business Administration
Major: Marketing
Minor: Advertising

SCHOLASTIC ACHIEVEMENTS:

- Dean's List — 2 semesters
- Graduated upper 10% of class

COLLEGE ACTIVITIES:

- Member, Marketing Club
- President, Advertising Club
- Editor, "Columbia Advocate"

JOB EXPERIENCE:
Summers 1989-1992

Havermeyer Corporation, Stamford, Connecticut
Advertising Department Assistant, part and full-time

PERSONAL:
Willing to relocate (prefer Northeast area)

REFERENCES:
Available upon request

George Reinhold
344 Benson Street
Greenwich, CT 07503
(203) 555-0200 [home]
(212) 555-8500 [message]

Objective: Growth Position in the Graphic Arts Field

Education:
1993   SCHOOL OF CREATIVE ARTS, White Plains, New York
                    A.A.S. degree in Commercial Art

                                Major Subjects:
                                •Introduction to Visual Arts   •Sculpture
                                •Painting   •Ceramics
                                •3-dimensional Structures   •Art History
                                •Life Anatomy   •Production

**Military
Experience:**
July 1987 to   UNITED STATES ARMY
February 1991   **Occupational Specialty** — Graphic illustrator, draftsman. Acted in
                    capacity of supervisor and coordinator of a divisional training aid
                    section encompassing charts, Vu-graphs, slides, manuals, pamphlets,
                    maps, design of statistical charts. Prepared quarterly reports for
                    conferences and briefings.

Special Skills: • Leroy Lettering   • Layout   • Training Aids
                        • Instant Lettering   • Silk Screen   • Dummies
                        • Prestype   • Charts, Graphs   • Light Boxes
                        • Plotting   • Paste-up   • Ozalid
                        • Illustration   • Mechanicals   • Transparencies

Experience:
Summers   CREATIVE ADVERTISING CO.
1992 to 1993   75 Warnock Street
                    New York, New York
                    Letterer and Chartist

ELAINE A. BRONSTEIN

13 Orange Drive   •   New Hyde Park, NY 11506   •   (516) 555-4389

MARKET RESEARCH ASSISTANT

JOB OBJECTIVE

A beginning position in the marketing department of an expanding organization with the purpose of eventually qualifying for general marketing or product management responsibilities.

EDUCATION

GRADUATE SCHOOL OF BUSINESS
UNIVERSITY OF PENNSYLVANIA, Philadelphia, PA
Candidate for M.B.A. concentrating in marketing.

Courses taken: Accounting, Economics, Marketing, Banking, and Quantitative Analysis.

Advanced courses taken: Introduction to Marketing Research, Marketing Management, International Trade and Finance, Sales Management, Consumer Motivation and Behavior, Management Strategy, and Policy.

CITY UNIVERSITY OF NEW YORK
New York, NY — 1993

• Received B.A. degree with honors in History.
• Graduated in top 6% of class.
• Made Dean's List 9 out of 12 terms.
• Elected to membership in Pi Gamma Mu,
   social science honor society.
• President of the Spanish club

EXPERIENCE
October to
December
1992

RYDER COMMUNICATIONS CORPORATION
220 Lexington Ave., New York, NY
Advertising agency market research assistant

Summers
1989 to
1992

CITY PARKS AND RECREATION DEPARTMENT
New Hyde Park, NY
Playground assistant

1985
and
1988

CAMP QUINIPET
Jennings Point, Shelter Island, NY
Senior camp counselor

Resume Review Form

When you have completed the final draft of your resume, check it carefully against each item of the checklist below. Rewrite it if you feel it does not meet any of the requirements.

It is important that your resume be as perfect as possible if it is to do the job it was designed to do—get you interviews.

Appearance

- ☐ Clear typeface
- ☐ Sharp reproduction
- ☐ Liberal spacing in margins and between paragraphs
- ☐ Headings capitalized
- ☐ Important points underlined
- ☐ Good-quality bond paper

Content (Make sure each item is covered.)

Identification

- ☐ Name
- ☐ Address
- ☐ Telephone number

Objective

- ☐ Title of position
- ☐ Specific goal

Education

- ☐ Name of school
- ☐ Dates of attendance
- ☐ Diplomas, certificates, or degrees
- ☐ Special honors or citations

Experience

- ☐ Dates of employment
- ☐ Company name
- ☐ Address
- ☐ Function of company (product or service)
- ☐ Your job title
- ☐ Description of your duties
- ☐ Special accomplishments and promotions

Miscellaneous

☐ Organizations

☐ Professional affiliations

☐ Availability for travel or relocation

☐ References (optional)

Writing

☐ Clear, concise style

☐ Correct spelling and punctuation

☐ Correct grammar

☐ Use of power verbs to describe duties and accomplishments

RESUME REMITTANCE CHART

FOR EFFECTIVE FOLLOW-UP, USE THIS FORM TO KEEP TRACK OF YOUR RESUMES AND COVER LETTERS

Date	Sent To	Name & Title	Position	Response/Follow-Up

Reentering the Job Market

If you are reentering the job market after many years at home, the job of preparing a resume is difficult. You cannot simply list your experience as is done in a chronological resume if your last job ended 10 years ago. Nor can you rely on paid experience. You must analyze the skills you have acquired during your "retirement" from the working world and incorporate them in your resume.

Have you been active in fund-raising affairs? Have you helped to write or edit the PTA newsletter? How about time spent planning or organizing youth activities? Or supervising volunteer activities at the local hospital? Make all of these activities count on your resume.

In preparing your resume, follow the format of the functional resume with the emphasis on your skills, aptitudes, and accomplishments. Lead off with a detailed summary of your experience—both paid and unpaid. Next, list the firms you have worked for, with a description of your duties and responsibilities in each position. Be sure to include relevant volunteer work in school or community activities.

Although most resumes should list dates of employment, it is better if you have been out of the job market for a number of years to leave out dates in your resume. Your main objective when reentering the job market after an absence is to get a face-to-face interview where you can sell your abilities to a prospective employer. Therefore, you should avoid mentioning anything in your resume that will stand in the way of that chance. A sample of a resume for an individual reentering the job market is on page 84.

An alternative approach for reentering the job market after an absence of many years is to construct a letter which describes your experience, qualifications, and skills in narrative form. Send this letter, instead of a resume, to present your qualifications to prospective employers. Save your resume for the job interview when you can explain your work record in person. A copy of this type of letter-resume is on page 85.

Sample Resume and Letter for Reentering the Job Market

SALLY DICKERSON
411 North 12th Street
Cleveland, Ohio 44136
(614) 555-2465

PUBLIC RELATIONS ASSISTANT

SUMMARY OF EXPERIENCE
- Customer relations
- Supervision of office personnel
- Developed system for efficient use of forms to control work flow
- Wrote correspondence
- Researched information for clients
- Kept accounts payable and accounts receivable records
- Prepared public relations materials for fund raising
- Worked with radio and TV stations for support of medical facility
- Assisted president of firm in all aspects of administration of real estate office

EMPLOYMENT
Roslyn Berks Health Center
1426 Euclid Avenue, Cleveland, Ohio
Public Affairs Assistant for health care center and treatment facility which performed services for 12,000 people. Responsibilities included:
- Providing information to residents and patients on the functions and activities of the center.
- Planning fundraising events with local radio and television stations to promote the center as a public service.
- Working with county officials in developing ongoing programs.

M.R. Flanders Company, Inc.
4967 Avenue A, Pittsburgh, PA
Assistant to the president of a small real estate office. In this position, was responsible for the day-to-day operation of the office, which included:
- Posting all checks and invoices to proper ledger.
- Supervising the typing of leases.
- Answering inquiries and complaints from customers and tenants.
- Showing properties to prospective buyers.
- Maintaining liaison with city building officials, construction companies, and suppliers.

EDUCATION
University of Pittsburgh — 3 years
Majored in English

Western Pennsylvania Business School — 1 year
Accounting and business procedures

Sally Dickerson
411 North 12th Street
Cleveland, Ohio 44136
(614) 555-2465

March 28, 19—

Standard Products, Inc.
1410 Berwick Street
Cleveland, Ohio 44178

Dear Sir or Madam:

I am replying to your advertisement in the *Cleveland Plain Dealer* for a public relations assistant.

As a former member of a local health care center which provides educational and informational aid to 12,000 community residents, I have participated in planning and implementing fundraising events, public affairs, and media coverage.

Although this was a voluntary, unpaid position, the experience has given me an extremely good background in all aspects of public affairs, including writing, editing, and researching. My administrative skills are excellent, as I previously have held a responsible office position with a real estate firm.

I would appreciate the privilege of an interview where I can have the opportunity of presenting my qualifications to you in person.

Thank you for your consideration.

Sincerely yours,

Sally Dickerson

Chapter 5

THE COVER LETTER

Now that you have composed a magnificent resume, how do you go about getting it into the hands of all those personnel managers who have not yet heard of your great talent? It would seem that the obvious answer is to put it into an envelope and deposit it in the nearest mailbox. This is a good idea if you're looking for the quickest way to get rid of it. But if you want to be sure your resume receives the attention it deserves, you have to add a letter of transmittal or cover letter. By itself your resume is like a news story without a headline or a picture without a caption. It must be identified, packaged, and directed to a specific reader.

The main function of the cover letter is to key your resume to a specific job. In addition, because it is addressed to an individual and signed by you, it adds a personal touch. As you will see by the samples on pages 89-98, cover letters are short, but must contain the following information:

Name and Title of Addressee

Once you know the name of the person to whom you are writing, a phone call to the company will get you his or her title. Omitting it will not have a detrimental effect on your chances, but it is better to include it.

Title of Position

The title of the position for which you are applying should be written under the salutation, or in the first paragraph. This is important, since the main purpose of your cover letter is to direct your resume toward a specific position.

Pinpoint Your Qualifications

Refer to the portions mentioned in your resume which have specific relevance to the requirements of the position for which you are applying. For example, if you are answering an ad for an accountant that specifically asks for manufacturing costs, you would point out in your cover letter any cost accounting background you might have. This information may be buried in the text of your resume, and reference to it in your letter would make you a stronger candidate for an interview.

Other Information

The cover letter is the place to include any personal information not shown in your printed resume. This includes such items as temporary telephone numbers, where messages can be left for you, and present and desired salary. However, mention salary only if it is requested in the advertisement, and if you do, be realistic. Keep in mind the level of your experience and the specifications of the position for which you are applying. Of course, everyone wants to improve his salary in a new job, but if you ask for an amount that is far beyond your present earnings or out of line with the requirements of the position, you will price yourself out of the job before you get an interview.

Salaries are usually based on two considerations. The first is your earnings. You may not consider this a fair criterion, especially if you feel that you are being underpaid, but most firms will key their offer, at least in part, to your current or most recent salary. Second, personnel managers generally know what they have to pay for certain levels of experience in a particular industry.

Your starting salary requirements are largely a matter of your personal needs, but you should be flexible. Consider the job and the company and try to project your earnings over the next few years. Are you better off with a larger salary in a dead-end job or a smaller salary in a job with a future? Think about it and add it up.

Sample cover letters for use in replying to classified advertising are shown on the following pages. Letters for the hidden job market will be found on pages 112-126.

DO'S AND DON'TS

DO address your letter to a single individual to avoid a "form letter" look. Use his or her title, and be sure to spell the name right.

DO illustrate your value to a prospective employer by using percentages and figures, if possible, when describing your accomplishments.

DO use active verbs to describe your duties and responsibilities. (See page 25)

DO keep your words simple and direct, and your sentences short.

DO check your letter carefully before mailing for possible spelling, punctuation or grammatical errors. Have another person read your letter. A fresh viewpoint can be helpful.

DO retain a copy of every letter you send, so that you will know what you wrote to each prospective employer. You may have to repeat facts and figures in an interview and you don't want to make any blunders.

DO keep track of where and when you send each letter and resume so that you can follow-up effectively.

DO keep your letter to a single page and leave lots of space all around.

DON'T fold your letter to fit a small personal envelope. Use business-size #10 envelopes only.

DON'T give reasons for leaving your job. Save them for the interview.

DON'T give your salary history. Again, this is a subject that should be saved for the interview. However, if an advertisement directs you to state your desired salary, show a range instead of a specific figure.

DON'T give opinions of former employers. Bad mouthing an ex-boss can backfire.

DON'T set conditions or make demands such as restrictions on travel or relocation.

DON'T mention benefits. It's far too early in the game.

Sample Cover Letters for
Replying to Classified Advertising

1419 N. 2nd Avenue
Staten Island, NY 10334
December 16, 19--

Advertiser
Box Y-6821
New York Times
New York, NY 10036

   RE: ADVERTISING PRODUCTION ASSISTANT

Gentlemen:

  In reply to your advertisement in the New York Times of December 14th, I am enclosing a copy of my resume.

  My education and experience in the field of graphic arts has provided me with a thorough knowledge of advertising production. My last position afforded an opportunity to become familiar with advertising agency traffic procedures.

  I believe my background fits your general requirements, and I would appreciate the opportunity of presenting my qualifications in a personal interview.

  Thank you for your consideration.

         Sincerely yours,

         Helen Kleeber
         (718) 555-9325

129 Radial Avenue
Bronxville, NY 10705
February 8, 19--

914-555-9401

Box Z-5467
WESTCHESTER TIMES
White Plains, New York

Gentlemen:

Your advertisement for a Marketing Trainee is exactly the kind of position I have been looking for.

I just graduated from Columbia University with a B.S. in Marketing and a minor in Advertising. I have very little experience, but I have lots of enthusiasm and a sincere desire to succeed in the field of marketing.

As requested in your advertisement, my resume is enclosed. I would appreciate the opportunity of presenting my qualifications in a personal interview.

Yours truly,

Leonore Rood

THOMAS HALSTEAD
1426 South Elm Street
San Francisco, CA 95318
415-555-3095

February 21, 19--

Box 1354
THE SAN FRANCISCO CHRONICLE
San Francisco, CA 95673

Re: Your advertisement for: Junior Cost
Accountant

As you can see by the enclosed resume, I have a degree in accounting plus 3 years of intensive experience with a large corporation.

In this position, I have participated not only in general accounting procedures, but have had the opportunity to work with the controller of the corporation in general audits and cost breakdowns.

My present firm is relocating to the east coast, and although they asked me to go with them, I cannot, for personal reasons, leave the San Francisco area at this time.

From the specifications listed in your advertisement I feel that I have the general qualifications and would appreciate the opportunity of a personal interview.

Yours very truly,

James Davis
1201 Peachtree Street
Houston, TX 75382
(713) 555-8900

December 23, 19--

Box C-1828
ARCHITECTURE MONTHLY
388 Madison Street
Chicago, IL 60924

Dear Sirs:

Your advertisement for a Chief Engineer interests
me very much.

I have had 15 years' experience as a construction
engineer, and for the past 6 years have held the position
of Chief Engineer. Due to the fact that my present firm
has been absorbed into another organization, I feel that
my future opportunities would be limited, and I am seeking a position with a greater challenge.

My present earnings are within the range of the
salary offered in your advertisement, and I would welcome
the opportunity to discuss my background and objectives
with you personally.

Yours very truly,

James Davis

February 18, 19--

Box X-2567
Chicago Tribune
Chicago, IL 60606

<u>Consumer Affairs Representative</u>

Gentlemen:

The qualifications listed in your advertisement in the February 17th issue of the Chicago
Tribune fit my background exactly.

For the past four years I have been in the
public relations department of a major pharmaceutical firm in which position I supervise
customer relations and consumer affairs activities.

In this capacity, I write and help produce
all of the company's communications which are
designed to improve relations between the firm,
the nearby community, and customers. This includes
pamphlets, brochures, speeches, publicity releases,
and special correspondence.

As you will see in the enclosed resume, I
have a degree in Journalism and while in college
I interned with a major advertising agency.

I would welcome the opportunity of an interview, where I can present samples of my work and
discuss in detail how my background and experience
in the corporate communications field can be of
value to you and your organization.

Your consideration of my qualifications for
this position will be most appreciated.

Yours truly,

Samantha Harding

1426 Farrell Ave.
Chicago, IL 60642
(315) 555-8694

FRANCIS POLANSKI
19 Kolbe Lane
Brooklyn, NY 11224
718-555-2598

August 16, 19--

Box 946
The Legal Journal
25 W. 16th St.
New York, NY 10016

Dear Advertiser:

The enclosed resume is submitted in response
to your recent advertisement for a Paralegal
Administrative Assistant.

Since your firm specializes in entertainment
law, I believe my experience in this area will be
of interest to you. As you will note in the enclosed resume, my last employer was a law firm re-
presenting clients in the record and video industries.
As an assistant to the senior partner I was involved
in the drafting of agreements for record and video
artists. I am familiar with licensing procedures,
union agreements, and general corporate matters.

I have excellent office skills including
proficiency with word processing equipment, and can
handle heavy responsibility.

Your consideration will be appreciated, and
I look forward to an early interview.

Sincerely yours,

FRANCIS POLANSKI

BEATRICE LETTERMAN
2694 Royer Street
Macon, Georgia 30247
(404) 555-5887

November 30, 19--

P.O. Box 5367
THE CREDIT REPORTER
256 West Peachtree St.
Atlanta, GA 30345

Gentlemen:

This is in response to your advertisement for a Credit Representative. As you will see by the enclosed resume, my experience is made to order for your position.

Here are some of the highlights of my background in the field of credit:

+ Responsible for the control and maintenance of over 5000 accounts for a major public utility.

+ Collected past due bills, resolved disputes, and recommended collection procedures.

+ Communicated with customers by telephone, and correspondence using techniques to maintain good customer relations.

I am accustomed to working in a fast-paced environment, and I believe I have the necessary skills to make a significant contribution to your credit staff.

Thank you for your consideration. I look forward to a personal interview.

Sincerely,

Beatrice Letterman

Elaine Neilson
3275 Farragut Ave.
Chapel Hill, NC 95123
(919) 555-4589

October 17, 19--

Mr. Frank Allen
Design Director
Folsom Textile Company
34 Raritan Street
Chapel Hill, NC 27456

Dear Mr. Allen:

I am a textile designer waiting to be discovered.

I cannot offer you experience, but I do have a
Bachelor of Fine Arts degree in Textile Technology
from the Philadelphia Textile Institute, and I have
been told by my instructors and certain biased
relatives that I do have talent.

Since your firm is recognized as a leader in the
production of a wide variety of domestics and other
textile products for home and industry, I would like
very much to be considered for a junior art position.

I would appreciate the opportunity of bringing in
my portfolio for your appraisal and consideration.

Sincerely,

Elaine Neilson

SANDRA LARCH
821 Ohio Street
Bryn Mawr, PA 19010
(215) 555-5833

November 20, 19--

Mr. Knute Donaldson
Corporate Communications Mgr.
American Health Care Institute
126 N. Broad Street
Philadelphia, PA

Dear Mr. Donaldson:

The current issue of <u>Healthways</u>, published by the National Association of Health Care Professionals, carried an article about the move of your national office to Philadelphia.

As a public relations specialist, I am interested in joining an organization involved in the health care field. With fifteen years of experience in communications, I can offer solid credentials in writing, editing, press relations and organizational skills.

I have an extensive portfolio of publications, articles, and press releases that I have produced over the years, and would appreciate the opportunity to present these to you as evidence of my creativity and competence in communications.

If your organization does not have an opening for a communications professional at this time, perhaps you could look at my material as a possibility for the future. In any event, I would be grateful for any advice you may be able to give me regarding my desire to move into the non-profit health field.

I will call you in a few days in the hope that you can see your way clear to arrange an interview.

Sincerely,

Sandra Larch

MICHAEL RICHMAN
2122 S. Beechwood Drive
Los Angeles, CA 90068

January 16, 19--

Box X4395
Los Angeles Times
Los Angeles, CA 90045

Dear Advertiser:

Your advertisement in the Los Angeles Times for a
Financial Systems Analyst caught my attention. As the
attached resume shows, I have the precise background
you seem to be looking for.

My total experience in financial systems encompasses over seven years, all of which were spent with
major financial institutions.

Here are a few of my accomplishments:

- Developed and implemented a system that enabled
  a bank equities department to operate more efficiently at a lower budget.

- Conducted time and motion studies which resulted
  in the installation of a new system for the
  transfer of data, effecting substantial annual
  savings.

- Instituted a training program for computer operators that resulted in an increase in output
  in the data entry department.

Your consideration of my qualifications for your
position is most appreciated. I will call you in a few
days in the hope of setting up an appointment.

Sincerely yours,

Michael Richman
(213) 555-6823

Part Two
Getting The Job

Chapter 6

IT'S LATER THAN YOU THINK

The only thing that vanishes faster than money is time, and both are short when you are looking for a job. Even if you do all the right things and your campaign is working, your job search can be long and arduous with unexpected road blocks and detours.

Your first task is to locate a company that has a job opening. That can consume from a few days to a month or more depending upon the state of the economy and your competition. Answering help wanted ads and sending your letters and resumes to prospects, places you at the mercy of the U.S. Postal Service, which hasn't won any medals for speed since the Pony Express. Also keep in mind that a reply to a box number goes to the newspaper first which then forwards it to the advertiser. From your mailbox to the company can take a week.

Your material then has to wend its way out of the corporate mailroom to the right department where it may marinate for a few more days. Should you hit the jackpot and receive an invitation to an interview, the appointed time can be the following week.

The interview seems to go well (at least from your viewpoint) and you are told to go home and wait for a call. In most cases if you take this advice seriously, be sure and lay in a good supply of rations. It may take some time. If the interview really did go well, you will probably be asked to come back for a second interview. Add another week or two . . . you get the picture. Of course, there's always the possibility that you get a job offer the first week. There's also the possibility that you will win first prize in the lottery. In case you're not that lucky, here are a few tips on how to organize your time.

Set Goals

There are only 480 minutes in an 8-hour day. If you are to attain your objective—to get a job as quickly as possible—you can't afford to waste a single one of them.

If you are now employed and looking for a new job, your time is seriously limited. Your paper work correspondence has to be done at home, interviews and telephone calls worked in during lunch periods or when your boss is on vacation or at the golf course. Unless your employer knows of your intentions and is cooperating with you, your search will have to take on some of the aspects of a CIA undercover operation.

If you are not employed, you also have a time problem. You have too much of it. Without the duties of a regular job with its regular hours plus those which you spend in commuting, time will lie heavily on your hands. It requires a tremendous amount of self-discipline to keep active when there is no one monitoring the results except yourself. One way to attain this self-discipline is to set daily quotas for your job hunting activities.

If you are totally immersed in your job hunting activities you will be busily engaged in a variety of tasks: researching companies, contacting trade associations and organizations for information, writing letters of all kinds, establishing contacts for networking, making telephone calls, and so forth. Without some planning and organization, you'll find yourself jumping haphazardly from one activity to another and not really getting the full benefits of any of them.

Here is how successful salespeople handle their working time. Faced with a long list of prospects to call on—old customers to be served, new firms to be contacted, telephone calls, follow-up letters, complaints, and a myriad of other details that have to be accomplished within a limited time, they divide their day into manageable segments. You can do the same. In addition to blocking out time for each activity, a good salesperson also sets a minimum number of calls he or she makes on prospects and customers every day, and sticks to it. This may seem like a lot of silly regimentation to the inexperienced, but look at the mathematics. Setting a quota to reach five prospects a day doesn't sound like much, but if done conscientiously it means 25 calls a week, 100 a month, 1200 a year. You can see the possibilities. Each individual can set different quotas depending on the time needed for each activity. But the system is only effective if the quota is met. It can be adjusted up or down until the right mix is set. The key is self-discipline. It's easy to set a quota. The tough job is forcing yourself to meet it. Undisciplined salespeople can be spotted easily. They're the ones with briefcases, sitting on park benches, figuring out the track odds or waiting on line at the local unemployment office.

You as a job-hunter can make good use of the successful salesperson's system. For example, if you are answering help-wanted advertising in your daily newspaper, set a quota for yourself of answering ten ads a week. You will be conducting a direct-mail campaign to selected firms. Discipline yourself to write at least two letters a day. Visit at least one new employment agency and contact one with whom you are already registered once a week.

By setting quotas and meeting them you will be pleasantly surprised at the cumulative effect of such a system within a few weeks.

A word of caution: don't set your quotas so high that you cannot meet them, but make them high enough to keep yourself busy.

Keep Office Hours

Since looking for a job should be considered a full-time job in itself, pretend you are working for a tough boss who demands punctuality and hard work.

The first rule is to start on time. This doesn't mean that you have to be out of the house every day at 9 A.M., but you should be working on something pertaining to your job search by that time instead of watching the latest disasters on the morning news. Leisurely breakfasts and vacation-like routines are out for the duration. Write the first letter of the day, mail a resume, call a prospect or an employment agency or go out for your first appointment.

Also, don't quit early in the afternoon because you have completed your scheduled activities by 3 P.M. Visit the public library and research some companies, or make an extra telephone call.

There's another benefit to be derived from keeping busy besides the practical one of getting a job sooner. It's hard not to become discouraged when you discover that your letters go unanswered and your telephone is not ringing. Setting and meeting quotas for activities allows you little time to get depressed or indulge in self-pity. It's also easier on your family if they don't have to see you moping around the house.

Chapter 7

HOW TO USE CLASSIFIED ADVERTISING

The classified section of your daily newspaper provides the quickest way of finding available positions in your area.

According to a recent survey conducted by the U.S. Department of Labor, sixty percent of employers polled reported that they hired through classified advertising.

The Sunday edition usually carries the most job openings. However, the serious job-seeker studies the help wanted columns every day, including Saturdays.

The most productive way to read this advertising is to study the entire section, circling every ad that offers even the remotest possibility even if it is not in your occupational specialty. Personnel people are not copywriters; you have to read between the lines to see what they are actually looking for. In addition, a job could be listed under the wrong heading—the result of carelessness on the part of the advertiser or the newspaper.

A Barometer of the Job Market

Reading *all* of the ads gives you the opportunity to study the job market in your field. Like most other markets, the job market operates on the principle of supply and demand. If, for example, there is a demand for accountants, you will see it reflected in the large number of accounting jobs listed. If you are an accountant, this means that your job search will be shorter, that you can afford to be more choosy and that you can negotiate your salary from a position of strength. On the other hand, if ads for your specialty are few and far between, you know you have to tighten up your search and work harder. You can't be too independent in your demands.

Classified advertising volume is taken very seriously by the Department of Labor. Corporations study classified advertising to pinpoint trends for future planning. A careful analysis of ads in your job field published in your area can also help you determine how you stand in the market with your background, skills, and experience.

When you have chosen those ads that you want to answer, cut them out, paste each on a card and place in a new manilla folder which will be your permanent record of transactions resulting from the individual ad.

Why Companies Use Box Numbers

There are three categories of classified ads—those run by companies with box numbers, those run by companies with their names and addresses, and those run by employment agencies. In most states where agencies are licensed, they are not permitted to use box numbers and are required to identify themselves as employment agencies.

Companies who use box numbers do so for several reasons. They may not want

103

their employees to know they are hiring. They may not want their competition to know they are hiring. They prefer to see what kind of people are available before they disclose their identity. Some companies who advertise do not have current job openings at all. Their purpose is to accumulate resumes for future vacancies.

The disadvantages in replying to a box number are obvious. You are revealing your work history, including your present employer, to unknown parties. If you don't receive an answer, you have no way to follow up. And if you answer your present employer's ad, you will have a lot of explaining to do very quickly.

Most companies do not acknowledge letters from applicants in whom they have no interest. Your letters and resumes go directly from the mailbox into oblivion. You never even get the chance to learn who turned you down.

Look for ads where companies sign their names. If they are not well-known, you can find out all you need to know about them through a directory available at your public library.

Timing Your Response

Contrary to what you may think, it is not a good policy to reply to a help wanted ad the same day it appears for the first time. We have all been brought up to believe that the early bird catches the worm. When it comes to answering ads, the early bird often gets lost in the crush. Personnel people, in general, when they see a very good applicant too early in the game, will almost always hold him or her in abeyance. Having a good applicant in hand at this stage, they can afford to take their time and see if they can do better, knowing that if they cannot, they still have the earlier applicant to fall back on. I suspect that if the ideal applicant comes up too soon, personnel managers get the impression that there are many capable, qualified people available—and may then take their time in choosing. So, do not sprint to the nearest mailbox to get your reply in the morning pickup.

Being the last to arrive at a party sometimes attracts more attention than being first. Keep in mind, however, that this ploy is not always guaranteed to work. If you are a really good applicant, your resume will receive a warm welcome whenever it arrives, but some personnel managers getting your answer to Sunday's ad on the following Friday may consider it tardy. So, do not wait too long and be the last one to get in. It has been my experience that resumes which are mailed to arrive in the company's office about one week after the ad runs seem to fare better in getting interviews. Remember also that when you are replying to a box number, your letter must go to the newspaper first, which then forwards it to the advertiser.

The Trade Press

Although your local newspaper is the handiest source of help wanted advertising, don't ignore the trade press.

Every industry has its own newspapers and magazines and most carry classified advertising. You should be reading your trade publications anyway for trends in your industry as well as other information that can be helpful in your search.

Trade magazines can generally be found at your local public library or ordered directly from the publishers. Answer their ads the same way you would answer those in a newspaper.

Self-Advertising

Another way you can use classified advertising is by placing your own ad in the "Positions Wanted" or "Situations Wanted" columns.

Although this requires a moderate cash investment, it is an avenue that should be explored. If it can get you one solid contact, it is worth it. Be prepared, however, to receive replies from insurance companies, brokerage houses, encyclopedia publishers, and other firms looking for commission salespeople. In addition, you may receive business opportunities propositions, mail-order gimmicks, and other questionable offers.

Chapter 8

THE HIDDEN JOB MARKET

Of all the job openings that occur each year, approximately seventy-five to eighty-five percent never reach the eyes and ears of the public.

They are filled without the benefit of advertising, employment agencies or head-hunters. They represent almost every occupation. How do these jobs get filled?

(1) From within the company. Most firms look to their present staff before going outside to recruit candidates.

(2) Personal recommendation and word of mouth. Jim Jones, VP for marketing for the AAA Manufacturing Company meets John Smith, advertising manager for the XYZ Company at an industry convention. During a conversation at dinner, Jim mentions one of his company's sales reps is retiring and they are looking for a replacement. John has a friend who is looking for a new connection. During dessert they exchange business cards and a week later an interview is arranged.

This happens frequently at vacation resorts, conventions, cocktail parties, and all kinds of affairs where executives gather for business or pleasure.

Many large companies have a policy requiring that a job be posted so that employees have an opportunity to apply for more responsible positions within the company, thereby saving the time, effort, and expense of recruiting from the outside.

How to Uncover the Hidden Jobs

This largely unknown and unpublished job market can be exposed. It takes time, lots of homework, and a moderate cash investment. The results can be worth it.

Personnel professionals and career counselors consider it to be one of the best methods of finding the right job. The major paths to this job market are:

- Skills marketing through direct mail
- Effective follow-up
- Use of specialized media
- Productive networking activities

The elements of a successful direct mail campaign are:

- The right mailing list
- A good resume
- A well-written cover letter

Each of these is vital. If one element is weak, the entire campaign will be weak. The key to your campaign, however, is the right prospect mailing list. The most effective resume and cover letter will be wasted if they do not reach the right person.

Finding the Right Mailing List

Almost every business, trade, industry, and professional organization is listed in one or more directories, other than the telephone book. These directories can be bought, borrowed or rented. Most are available in public libraries. They contain very detailed information such as annual sales volume, products or services, names and titles of officers, plant facilities, corporate affiliations, and a host of other useful information.

If you aren't sure which directory to use, there is even a Directory of Directories (See Appendix 5) to help you choose. With all this information available to you, you can pick and choose the people you want to reach in those companies for whom you would like to work.

If you wish, you can buy these volumes directly from the publishers. They range in cost from approximately fifty to several hundred dollars depending upon their size and scope, Keep in mind, however, that directories are updated constantly. Having a private reference library would be very convenient but it will become obsolete quickly. Most libraries receive current editions.

A list of directories can be found under "Sources of Information by Occupation" on page 159, and "General Business Directories" on page 171.

How to Use Your Directory

From the directory you have chosen for your mailing list, enter the name, address and telephone number of the person you want to reach for each company on an index card. The individual you choose should be the head of the department where your experience and background are likely to be needed. Never send your material to the personnel manager (unless you are looking for a job in the personnel department). Personnel usually gets into the act only after all other recruiting efforts have failed. Unless you are lucky enough to have your resume and letter arrive at the time the personnel department has a job requisition that just fits your background, it may be relegated to the nearest hold file, or worse, the round file underneath the desk.

In using direct mail remember that you are not responding to an advertisement. You don't know if a position exists. Your objective is to convince someone that you can be an asset to their company. You are not asking for a job. You are asking for an interview.

If the directory does not list the department head, telephone the firm. Tell the operator that you want to send some informational material to the controller, advertising manager, purchasing director or head of whatever department you are seeking to reach. Ask for the person's name and title. Do not tell the operator that you are looking for a job, or you will be immediately shunted to personnel. It's a good idea to call for this information even if the name *is* listed to make sure that the person is still there. Directories take many months to compile and frequent personnel changes within a company make accuracy difficult.

What to Send

Should your initial contact in a mail campaign be by resume and cover letter or letter alone? Most personnel experts favor sending a resume accompanied by a short cover letter. Your letter should consist of two main themes: (1) What are your accomplishments and (2) How can they be of value to the targeted company.

There are two categories of applicants who may find it more effective to send a letter without a resume, and they are at opposite ends of the experience and salary scale. If you are an executive earning $75,000 or over, you should address your letter to the president or executive vice president of the company. The letter should present the highlights of your background and experience including a description of some of your major accomplishments, plus the reasons why you want to work for the company. It should not include a chronological listing of your jobs—this is the function of your resume.

If you are just out of school and looking for your first full-time job, your resume will probably look like everyone else's in the same situation. At this stage, all you have to offer is your name, address, telephone number, and education. You could fill space with gems like: "Hobbies: sailing, mountain climbing, reading, and partying." Or, "waiting on tables at Ptomaine Tom's Diner" or "checkout clerk at Herman's High Price Supermarket," but they won't do much for your resume.

Again, do not address your letter to the personnel manager, but rather to the head of the department in which you want to begin your career. Since your experience is minimal, concentrate on the high points of your education. List any awards, scholarships or honors earned. If you served an internship, mention the name of the company and the nature of the work. State your career objective and try to include a few facts that you know about the firm as a sign that you were interested enough to do some research.

At the end of the letter, ask for the opportunity of presenting yourself and your resume at a personal interview.

Follow-Up

About ten days after your initial mailing, telephone the person to whom you addressed your letter. It's a good idea to call before 8 A.M. or after 5 P.M. Most managers arrive early and leave late. If the receptionist or secretary picks up the telephone, you may have a hard time getting through. It's their job to screen calls, and yours will probably be considered expendable.

When you do get your party, be positive. Don't apologize for the call. For instance: "Hello, Mr. Smith, this is Mary Jones. I'm following up on the letter I sent to you on March 15th. If you remember, I was with Franklin Research Company for the past four years as a financial analyst and I believe that my background could be of value to your firm. If you could spare a few minutes, I would like to stop up to see you and get some advice about getting relocated."

You're not actually asking Mr. Smith for a job, but you have made him aware that you did send him a letter and/or a resume. You have also reminded him of your background in case he has forgotten your letter, and you have complimented him by asking for his expertise in helping you with your job search. If his response is completely negative, go on to the next prospect. Don't brood over it. If you keep sending out your letters and following up, you will definitely get some invitations to an interview and that is your major objective.

Use the Media

One of the most productive sources of job prospects can be found in business news. Yet many job-hunters do not use it. The most obvious source is your daily newspaper. Here you will find information about companies coming into your city, new businesses starting up, new leases signed by local firms, announcements of personnel promotions and transfers.

Business and financial magazines provide a gold mine of information available for prospecting. Both the financial pages of newspapers and magazines contain news about mergers and acquisitions, plus important information about individual companies and industries, such as trends, sales figures, new products, plants and facilities, and personnel changes. Look for news of promotions. When a new manager takes over a department, some reorganization usually follows. Send a note of congratulations, enclosing a copy of the announcement. Everyone likes to see his or her name in print. They may not be aware of the publicity which is usually sent out to the media by the public relations department. It's a great way to introduce yourself and make a new contact.

Networking

Personal contacts are obviously a rich source of prospects. Have you ever made a list of every person you know? You will be surprised at how many friends and acquaintances you have in addition to your relatives. How well you know them doesn't matter. Make three separate lists as follows:

> *List #1*—Everyone you know, however slightly, who works in your field. This includes former employers, members of your business or professional association, past or, if still employed, present co-workers who will keep your confidence. This is your "best chance" list.
> *List #2*—Everyone who provides you with some professional service—your accountant, attorney, stockbroker, insurance expert, doctor, dentist, clergyman.
> *List #3*—Relatives, friends, acquaintances, former teachers, school placement counselors.

Each has a circle of his or her friends and acquaintances and relatives, many of whom are employed and in business. Help can come from the most unexpected sources when you are looking for a job. Networking can be compared in a sense to throwing a stone into a lake and watching the ripples grow wider and wider.

Contact each one starting with List #1 and ask for a personal appointment at home, the office or for lunch. Avoid stating your business on the telephone. It's too easy for them to request that you send a resume. Ask for a few minutes of time for some personal advice.

When you meet each contact, do not immediately offer your resume. Don't even bring it with you. When you get home, write a short note of thanks and enclose three copies of your resume.

A final word about contacts—especially business contacts. Don't push too hard. The first reaction to a request for help is flattering. A telephone call a few weeks after the first meeting is in order. But unless the person is a close personal friend or a relative, further contact may be counterproductive. After a while, conversation can become a little forced and embarrassing to the person who was asked for help, but is unable to give it. Play it by ear—you'll know when it's time to turn off the pressure.

Conventions and Trade Shows

If you're not a member of a trade or professional association covering your industry or occupation, you should be. Call or write your association and request membership information. They will send you a kit containing all you need to know about joining.

Most organizations operate placement services for members and nonmembers alike. Members receive magazines, bulletins, newsletters, and other material designed to keep them informed on news about the industry. They contain news about personnel changes, promotions, transfers, mergers, relocations, and other information that you will need in your job search.

If possible, attend every trade show or convention that you can. The investment you make in travel and hotel charges can pay off handsomely in making important contacts. Some or all of the expenses you incur in looking for a job can be deducted for income tax purposes.

At these business gatherings you will meet people who can prove to be vital links in your chain of contacts. Bring a supply of copies of your resume. Let people you meet know that you are in the job market. You will discover that most of them will be sympathetic and receptive to your problem since they will have been in the same boat themselves at one time or another. Conventions of sales people are particularly good for networking. They come into daily contact with a variety of companies and are an excellent source of inside information.

Most companies display their products at exhibit booths at trade shows. Visit and talk to the sales people manning these booths. Leave your card and resume. Everybody is a prospect, and the informal atmosphere provides easy access to people who, at the office, wouldn't give you the time of day.

Ask for a business card from everyone you speak to. When you arrive back home, follow up with a letter expressing your pleasure on meeting him or her and including a reminder of your continuing job search.

Sample Cover Letters for
the Hidden Job Market

JAMES FRANKEL
81 Pitt Street
Atlanta, GA 30318
404-555-8985

January 12, 19--

Mr. Victor Bradley
Director of Purchasing
1800 Lawrence Avenue
Atlanta, GA 30345

Dear Mr. Bradley:

     As you may know, my present firm, National
Laramie Corporation, has merged with the Midway
Atlantic Company. As a result my position in
their purchasing department has been eliminated.

     As you can see by the enclosed resume my
background in purchasing includes over six years
of diversified experience. I am thoroughly familiar
with supplier relations and purchasing procedures.

     In my present position I helped institute an
inventory control system which was responsible for
savings of over $40,000 annually. In addition
I originated and implemented a work-flow procedure
which eliminated duplication of effort and resulted
in a smoother and more rapid system of receiving
ordered material.

     Since your firm is a leader in the industrial
equipment field, I would like to be considered
for a position in either your purchasing, distribution or inventory control department.

     I would welcome the opportunity to have a personal
meeting with you in which I can present more detailed
information on how I can contribute to your company.

                    Sincerely yours,

SEYMOUR DAVIDSON
37-54 N. Roosevelt Boulevard
Dallas, TX 75321
(214)555-8931

January 19, 19--

Dear John,

Due to a merger, my position with the American
Toy Corporation has been eliminated, and I find myself
in the market for another job.

I have enclosed a copy of my resume to bring you
up to date on my activities to the present time.

Any ideas or recommendations that you can come
up with would certainly be helpful in my search for a
new connection.

As always, your friendly interest will be
appreciated.

Cordially,

45 West 75th Street
New York, NY 10023
November 15, 19--

Mr. Arthur Bradley
Personnel Manager
Warwick, Vanderbilt, Inc.
91 Wall Street
New York, NY 10016

Dear Mr. Bradley:

The enclosed resume is submitted for your consideration.

I am a recent college graduate with a B.S. in Accounting and an M.B.A. in Finance and I am seeking a position as a management trainee in this field.

If your firm has any suitable openings at this time, I would welcome the opportunity to present my qualifications in a personal interview.

Should there be no immediate interest, I would appreciate your retaining my resume for future reference.

Sincerely yours,

Shirley Roth

212-555-6700

Ronald Nelson
635 E. 18th Street
Brooklyn, NY 11204

April 18, 19--

Mr. Harvey Fieldstone
Director of Personnel
Foxline Manufacturing Co., Inc.
Astoria, New York   12136

Dear Mr. Fieldstone:

I am an experienced Purchasing Agent whose
position has just been phased out as a result of a
merger.

Since your firm is a leader in the manufacture
of electric products and enjoys an excellent reputa-
tion in the field, I would like to be considered for a
position in your purchasing department.

As you can see by the enclosed resume, I have
a solid background in the purchasing of all raw materials
related to the manufacture of electrical equipment
and have been instrumental in saving my previous
company over $200,000 during the past three years
through efficient purchasing practices.

I would appreciate the opportunity of meeting
with you personally to present my qualifications in
more detail.

Thank you for your kind consideration.

Sincerely,

Ronald Nelson
718-555-2967

201-555-1281   Joan Swanson
                                2711 Northview Road
                                Little Ferry, NJ 07172

                                January 4, 19--

Mr. Lawrence Jones
Creative Director
White, Lipped & Trembling, Inc.
425 Fifth Avenue
New York, NY 10022

Dear Mr. Jones:

     You will note from the enclosed resume that I
have had considerable experience as a copywriter, and
I am hoping that my background will be of some
interest to you.

     May I have the opportunity of discussing the
possibility of a position with your agency? I have
a complete portfolio of my work.

     If an interview is not warranted at this time,
I would appreciate your keeping this resume in your
file for any future openings which may occur.

                                Yours truly,

Robert J. Porter
41 Bow Lane
Norfolk, VA 24557

(703-555-2457)

April 15, 19--

Mr. James Farmer, VP
Newport National Bank
215 Arlington St.
Norfolk, VA 24562

Dear Mr. Farmer:

I am a commercial loan officer with eight years of banking experience.

Because my present employer is a small organization which offers limited opportunity for growth, I am seeking a position which will enable me to use my experience and knowledge to its fullest advantage. As a recognized leader in the field of commercial banking, your organization is the kind of firm I would like to be associated with.

I have a B.A. degree in finance from the University of Pennsylvania and an M.B.A. from the Wharton School of Finance. My experience includes two years as a financial analyst and four years as a commercial loan officer. I am thoroughly familiar with all phases of commercial banking operations.

A resume is enclosed for your consideration. I would welcome the opportunity of meeting with you or a member of your staff to present further details of my education and experience and to explore ways that I can be of value to your organization.

I look forward to hearing from you.

Yours very truly,

Robert J. Porter

FRANKLIN HUDSON
1261 Clay Avenue
Chicago, Il 60616
(315) 555-2387

November 21, 19--

Mr. Gerald Harrington
Harring, Silver & Forbes
1456 Madison Street
Chicago, Il 60645

Dear Mr. Harrington:

I am in need of some personal advice. Because of
your standing in the financial community, I am taking
the liberty of calling upon you for your professional
counsel. Even though we are not acquainted, I am
hoping you can give me a moment.

For some time, I have been grappling with a
critical career decision. By mutual agreement, my
present employer, Latrex Corporation, and I have decided to part. I am leaving on amicable terms, and
the company is fully supporting me in my job search.

I am a strong results-oriented financial executive, with across-the-board P&L experience. What
I am trying to do is focus on those most critical
aspects of my background and your intuitive sugges-
tions and recommendations would be invaluable to me.

I assure you that this is not an application
for employment and I do not approach you for this
purpose. My only reason for attaching my resume is
to summarize my experience should you be in a position to respond to my request.

I hope to have the opportunity of a short meeting
at your convenience, and I look forward to hearing
from you.

Sincerely yours,

```
                        LEONARD ROTH
                       14 MacArthur Road
                     San Francisco, CA 94117


                                        March 23,



Mr. James Radziwell
Creative Director
Friedman Forrester Agency
212 Market St.
San Francisco, GA 95176

Dear Mr. Radziwell:

The enclosed article regarding your new appointment
appeared in this week's edition of Advertising Age.
May I offer my congratulations?

Since the announcement also mentions the recent ac-
quisition of several new accounts by your agency,
I am wondering whether you contemplate increasing
your staff to service this new business.  If so,
I would very much like to be considered for a posi-
tion with your art department.

Until recently I was an assistant art director
for a major agency assigned to two large packaged
goods accounts.  I have won several awards for my
work and I would like to show my portfolio and
reels to you at your convenience.  They contain
samples of a variety of advertisements designed for
diversified print and broadcast media.

If there is nothing available in your department now,
I would appreciate your accepting my resume for
any future position that may occur.

With all best wishes for success in your new posi-
tion, I am

                                    Sincerely yours,


(415) 555-6837              Leonard Roth
```

ELAINE NELSON
2635 Walnut Street
Philadelphia, Pa 19113
215-555-4756

December 18, 19--

Mr. Frederich Marker
Director of Operations
Northeast Bank & Trust Co.
2631 W. 3rd Street
Valley Forge, Pa. 19547

Dear Mr. Marker:

The 1990s represent a unique challenge
to banking and financial institutions, both
domestic and multinational. As a result, more
and more companies are seeking solutions that
involve sound financial planning and management.

I believe that my education and training
in financial planning will enable me to make a
significant contribution to your organization.
As a recent graduate of the University of
Pennsylvania with a degree in Finance, I have
worked for the past two summers on a part-
time basis in a variety of business environments.
I have also served an internship with a public
accounting firm. These experiences have given
me the opportunity to use my academic training
in the real world of business.

I am 24 years old and looking for a bottom-
rung opportunity in the financial services industry.
I would welcome the opportunity of meeting you
or a representative of your firm so that I may
present my qualifications in person.

Thank you for your interest and consideration.

Sincerely,

Joseph Resnick
2741 Van Ness Expressway
Jenkintown, PA 19134

February 1, 19--

Mr. Robert L. Ganen, President
Grafton Manufacturing Company, Inc.
4235 Central Avenue
Philadelphia, PA 19356

Dear Mr. Ganen:

I read recently in Business Digest magazine
of the expansion of your company's sales operations
and your plans to create a new position of sales
director. If this position is still open, I would
appreciate your considering me for it.

My total sales experience encompasses 15
years, the last 5 of which have been as sales manager of a major manufacturer of packaged goods.

I am enclosing a resume of my qualifications
for your review, and I would appreciate a personal
interview with you in order to discuss my application further.

Very truly yours,

Joseph Resnick
(215) 555-2354

BERNICE WRISTON
4116 Wythe Circle
Boston, MA 02171
(617) 555-4086

April 4, 19--

Ms. Catherine Fenderman
VP, Director of Marketing
CRS Pharmaceutical Corp.
2662 E. Third St.
Boston, MA 02158

Dear Ms. Fenderman:

In the current issue of Sales and Marketing
Magazine, there is an item announcing your firm's
move to this city from St. Louis. The article
further stated that your sales department would
be expanding its staff.

I would very much like to be considered
for a junior sales position with your organization. I graduated from Boston College with a
B.S. in Marketing, and I am interested in pursuing
a sales career in the health care industry.

While in college I was the campus representative for a major cosmetic company. I like selling
and believe I can develop into a productive member
of your marketing staff.

I will contact your secretary in a few days
in the hope that you can spare a few minutes of
your time to allow me to present my qualifications
in person.

Very truly yours,

LAWRENCE GEOGHAN
1620 W. 34d St.
Chicago, IL 60641

(312) 555-4573

November 3, 19--

Mr. Frank Costello
Sales Manager
Ramci Corporation
1820 Lakeside Avenue
Chicago, IL 60634

Dear Frank:

Just as everything seemed to be going so well in my job, the roof fell in. Last week the company announced it was closing its Chicago plant. This sudden and unexpected development means that I am now back in the job market.

I have already lined up a couple of interviews here in town, but knowing how uncertain job hunting can be, I can use all the contacts I can get.

You know my record as a salesman. If you hear of any possibilities in your travels, I would certainly appreciate hearing about them.

As soon as I rewrite my resume, I will send you a copy to bring you up to date on my recent activities.

Cordially,

344 Benson Street
Greenwich, CT 07503
February 23, 19--

Mr. John Moreland
Art Director
Clayton, Brown & Forster, Advertising
386 Madison Avenue
New York, NY 10023

Dear Mr. Moreland:

I am a recent art school graduate and am seeking a beginner's position in the art department of a
large advertising agency.

Although my experience is limited to summer
employment and the military service, I have a complete portfolio showing samples of work that I have
done. This includes layout, pasteups and mechanicals,
lettering, and illustrations.

I would like to be considered for a position
with your firm and would be happy to present my
samples for your consideration.

A resume is enclosed for your information.
Thank you for your interest.

                                    Yours very truly,

203-555-8910   George A. Reinhold

MARCIA ALLEN
231 Franklin Street
Indianapolis, IN 46204
(317) 555-4765

November 16, 19--

Mr. Jack Andrews
Office Manager
Verity Advertising Agency
1465 N. Arlington Street
Indianapolis, IN 46204

Dear Mr. Andrews:

I am an experienced Word Processor with excellent skills. Due to the relocation of my last employer, I am seeking a new position.

For the past six years I have been employed as a secretary and general office assistant, and I am thoroughly familiar with the following word processing programs:

- WordStar 5.5
- WordPerfect 5.1
- MultiMate
- Microsoft Word
- Lotus 1-2-3

In addition, I can take shorthand at 110 words per minute and type at 80 words per minute.

As you can see by the enclosed resume, I have had diversified experience, and feel confident that I can be a valuable asset to your organization.

I would appreciate the opportunity of meeting you and presenting my qualifications at a personal interview. I can be reached at (317) 555-4765.

Sincerely,

Marcia Allen

JOHN A. RAWLINGS

133 Pine Avenue
Ridgefield, NJ 07932
(201) 555-2376

December 31, 19--

Ms. Francine Siddel
VP, Director of Human Resources
Aztec Industries, Ltd.
65 E. 54th Street
New York, NY

Dear Ms. Siddel:

This is in response to your advertisement in the December issue of <u>The Journal of Personnel Management</u> for an Employment Manager.

My background, as shown on the enclosed resume, seems to fit your requirements exactly, especially my experience in wage and salary administration. Other relevant achievements include:

* Created college recruitment program to attract top graduates for management training.

* Established wage and salary standards for exempt and non-exempt personnel.

* Administered a formal personnel policy program including establishment of performance review and incentive programs.

I can be reached at (201) 555-2376 and am available for an interview at any time that is convenient for you.

Yours truly,

John Rawlings

Chapter 9

HOW TO CHOOSE AND USE EMPLOYMENT AGENCIES

Employment agencies fill thousands of jobs almost every day in almost every occupation. A quick study of the classified help-wanted advertising pages in your local newspaper shows that a high percentage of the advertised openings are listed by agencies. Companies of all sizes allocate a substantial part of their recruitment budgets to paying agency fees. Employment agencies must be doing something right.

To get the most benefits from an employment agency you should know what its functions are and what it can and cannot do for you. Here are some facts about employment agency services.

- Agencies can save you time by getting you quick interviews and immediate feedback on their results.
- Many companies use agencies exclusively to fill their jobs, which are not advertised by the employer or publicized in any way to the general public.
- Your application becomes part of the agency's permanent active file, so you don't have to reapply for every opening that comes up.
- An agency protects your identity. You learn the name of the employer before applying for the job. You may not want certain firms to know that you are on the job market.
- An agency represents many companies who list their jobs regularly. You are exposed to more positions than you could possibly uncover yourself.
- Agencies can help coach you on what to say and how to conduct yourself during an interview.
- If your resume needs improving, a counselor can call your attention to its weaknesses and help you to correct them.
- Agency service is usually free to applicants, but in those instances where you may have to pay a fee, you are under no obligation until and unless you accept a position through their efforts.
- Agencies are not in the business to find you a job. Their function is to fill a job for their client companies. In order to keep them happy and retain their business, agencies work harder for employers than they do for applicants.
- Agency counselors work on a commission basis. They get a percentage of the fee when they fill a position. Human nature being what it is, as an applicant, you are either money in the bank or you're not. This leads to quick judgments. Experienced counselors have developed a knack of separating the easy placements from the hard ones. If you don't fit a set of exact job specifications, you don't get the referral. There are exceptions. You may be among the fortunate few who may find a counselor who really cares about your problem and who will take the time to advise you and make a real effort to place you in the right job.

- Companies retain agencies for the purpose of screening out people— and not always on the basis of experience or qualifications. Unfortunately some firms use agencies for the purpose of circumventing the various antidiscrimination laws. Older applicants in particular find less than enthusiastic reception at many agencies.
- An agency may try to sell you a job that you really don't want. In order to make the placement, unscrupulous counselors may withhold information or lie about the advancement opportunities or other important aspects of the position. Female applicants, particularly, are often encouraged to take interviews on jobs which turn out to be no more than clerical or secretarial in order to satisfy the large demand for people with office skills.

How to Find the Right Agency

A good way to choose an agency is to study the classified pages of your daily newspaper, and note those agencies that consistently advertise jobs in your field. You will notice over a period of time that agencies tend to specialize.

Another way to choose an agency is to get a recommendation from a company. Call the personnel manager of any well-known firm in your area and ask for a recommendation of an agency. You will probably get the name of one or more agencies that the firm does business with. Then call the agency and tell them that they were recommended by their client, mentioning the name of the person with whom you spoke. The agency will roll out the red carpet for you.

How to Make the Best Use of Your Agency

One of the major advantages of using an employment agency is that you have the opportunity to ask questions that you may be reluctant to ask at a company interview. You can safely inquire as to the benefits a company offers. A counselor who is doing his job should know what the client has to offer in the way of fringe benefits. You also have the advantage of being able to discuss your salary requirements and receive advice as to how much leverage you might have in salary negotiations. An employment agency can give you information about a prospective employer that you might find difficult to obtain elsewhere.

Here is a tip. If you want to get a little extra effort out of your agency, write your counselor a personal note of thanks the next day. Most agency counselors are under a lot of pressure. They are extremely busy people who are harassed by both employers and applicants. Any small courtesy, such as a thank-you note, can do wonders for their egos and make friends for you.

Use Agencies Early

Many job-hunters exhaust other sources before trying an agency. This is a mistake. You may feel that by diligently writing letters, answering ads, and pounding the sidewalks, you will get your job without the help of any agency. You could be right. But when you consider that an agency works on your behalf without charge, it doesn't make sense not to use it right away.

The Public Employment Service

The largest chain of employment agencies is operated by the U.S. Employment Service. A division of the Department of Labor, it shares funding and responsibilities with state employment offices. The service is free and available to everyone.

The State Employment Service has two functions: the first is to determine eligibility for and administer unemployment benefits. The second is to find jobs for those on their rolls. In a move to improve their services, the State Employment Service has established professional placement centers in many areas where executives and management personnel can be interviewed in a more professional setting.

Vocational testing is also provided at no cost. Veterans of the armed forces receive special treatment and disabled veterans are entitled to preferential services.

Career Counselors

During your job hunt you will notice that your newspaper carries advertising by a variety of companies offering career and job counseling services. These ads are enticing. Many appear to promise high-paying positions. You will get plenty of advice, but you won't get a job. You will, however, be asked to sign an agreement to pay a substantial fee which can go as high as several thousand dollars with few or no guarantees. These firms should be approached with extreme caution. Career counselors are not in the business of finding jobs, although their advertisements often leave that impression. What they will do is prepare your resume and cover letter, analyze your experience and background, and conduct interview rehearsals. They will also offer aptitude and psychological testing. They may attempt to get you interviews by sending your resume to a list of firms who may or may not have a job opening.

Some of these services are staffed by people with professional experience and credentials. Others are no more than boiler room operations with personnel only interested in furthering their own careers. You will be asked to sign a contract. Read it carefully so that you know exactly what you are getting and how much it will cost. Look for guarantees or refund provisions. Better yet, get your lawyer to read it and check the firm with your Better Business Bureau.

Chapter 10

JOB HUNTING ON THE INTERNET

A new national interest has burst on the scene over the past few years and has led to the creation of a whole new pastime. This new development is called the Internet, and it has turned the personal computer into a global information superhighway. This chapter will explain how the Internet can also be your road to a new job or career.

It is estimated that there are 20 to 30 million users of the Internet, with new users coming on-line daily. The Internet has become the dominant channel for the exchange of information among individuals, government agencies, libraries, schools and universities, corporations, professional societies, and private and public organizations of all kinds.

How to Use Your Computer to Find the Job You Want

Travelers on this electronic highway can explore exotic and unfamiliar places, establish contact with interesting people, talk in "real time" to people with similar interests, and acquire information that can help in their daily personal and business activities—electronically, without ever leaving home. For the job hunter, the Internet is a gold mine waiting to be tapped.

What's available on the Internet to help you find a job or plan a career? You can scan the Internet want ads and post your resume. You can check out industry profiles by accessing the U.S. Small Business Administration's statistics for all fifty states. You can access individual job postings or gather a whole variety of general employment information. Employers, recruiters, and executive search firms all use the Internet to recruit new employees.

Accessing the Internet for the first time may be frustrating for the neophyte, but you don't have to be a rocket scientist to get a handle on it. There is plenty of information available to make it easier for newcomers to participate. Consult one or two of the books about the Internet listed at the end of this chapter.

To begin your electronic job search, you will need a computer with modem, communications software, and a subscription to one or more on-line services such as CompuServe, America Online, Prodigy, Delphi, or Genie. On page 133 you will find a list of the major on-line services which, in addition to providing access to the Internet, offer a variety of software programs on disks and CD-ROMs designed specifically to help you get started in your electronic job hunt.

Job Hunting Programs

The following is a small sample of the programs available. Many others are described in the books and directories listed at the end of the chapter. They include disks, CD-ROMs, and Bulletin Board Systems (BBS). Software prices are generally moderate while BBS's services are free.

Dr. Job offers information on how to find a job, prepare a resume, change or advance your career, and much more. Presented in a question and answer format, Dr. Job is available through Genie.

Company Analyzer is a database providing extensive reports on over 10,000 public U.S. companies, including profile, earnings, growth potential and more. Company Analyzer is available through CompuServe.

Job Power Source is an interactive CD-ROM which includes information from *Occupational Outlook Handbook* and other books and periodicals published by the U.S. Bureau of Labor Statistics. The program presents video clips of job-searching techniques and features interactive worksheets focusing on job-hunting skills and career goals. Available from: Infobusiness, Inc., 887 S. Orem Blvd., Orem, UT 84058. Phone: 1-(800)-657-5300.

Encyclopedia of Associations is a CD-ROM providing access to information on organizations of all kinds: national, regional, state, and local. Available from: Gale Research, 835 Penobscot Building, Detroit, MI 48226. Phone: 1-(800)-877-4253.

The Perfect Resume is a career placement registry in which job hunters can post their resumes for examination by employers. This registry is available through Dialog.

On-line Classified Ads features classified ads for job-hunters nationwide. These are available through CompuServe, Genie, and Prodigy.

Computer Bulletin Board Systems (BBS) are communication programs that allow computer owners to use the telephone lines to post and read messages. These boards, used as a research source, can maximize your career strategy and make your job search more effective. Electronic bulletin board systems are run by individuals, corporations, government agencies, and business and professional organizations which disseminate information to the general public.

Select Phone is a CD-ROM program containing names, addresses, and phone numbers for over eight million businesses in the United States. Contact: Pro CD, Inc., 232 Rosewood Drive, Danvers, MA 01923. Phone: 1-(508)-750-0000.

Occupational Outlook Handbook, produced annually by the U.S. Department of Labor, Bureau of Labor Statistics, is available on CD-ROM. It describes over 250 occupations in detail—covering about 104 million jobs or 85 percent of all jobs in the nation. Information about each occupation includes nature of the work, working conditions, number of people employed, location of the jobs, job outlook, training, qualifications and advancement, earnings, related occupations, and sources of additional information. It is available from local U.S. Government Printing Office outlets or from your local office of the U.S. Bureau of Labor Statistics.

The Worldwide Resume/Talent Bank Service is a resume posting service in which job seekers can enter their resumes into an electronic database containing thousands of resumes of professionals in all career fields nationally and around the world. Available from: Gonyea & Associates, Inc., 3543 Enterprise Road East, Safety Harbor, FL 34695. Phone: 1-(813)-725-9600.

Resumaker is a software program to help job seekers compose resumes and cover letters. The job seeker enters data into specific types of resumes, and the program formats and produces the resume that best fits the user's needs. Also included is a library of cover letters, "thank you" notes, a built-in word processor, spell checker, and address book. Available from: Individual Software, Inc., 5870 Stonehenge Drive #1, Pleasanton, CA 94588. Phone: 1-(800)-822-3522.

American Yellow Pages is a CD-ROM containing more than 10 million businesses by city, state, county, and zip code. Available from: American Business Information, 5711 S. 86th Circle, P.O. Box 27347, Omaha, NE 68127. Phone: 1-(412)-593-4595.

The Directory of Executive Recruiters is provided on disks, DOS only. This directory is a list of over 2000 recruiting firms and offices nationally and worldwide, listed by specialty and by geographic location. Available from: Kennedy & Kennedy, Inc., Templeton Road, Fitzwater, NH 03447. Phone 1-(603)-585-2200 or 1-(603)-585-6544.

On-line Career Center is a database of career related information including employment ads. For access information, contact OCC at 3125 Dandy Trail, Indianapolis, IN 46214. Phone: 1-(317)-293-6499.

Commercial On-line Communications Services

The following is a list of computer network services. Obtain membership information, technical requirements, and usage rates by writing or calling.

AMERICA ONLINE
8619 Westwood Center Drive
Vienna, VA 22182
800-827-6364

COMPUSERVE
5000 Arlington Centre Blvd.
Columbus, OH 43222
800-848-8199

DIALOG INFORMATION SERVICES
3460 Hillview Ave.
Palo Alto, CA 94303
800-3-Dialog

GENIE
GE Information Services
PO Box 6403
Rockville, MD 20850
800-638-9636

DELPHI NETWORK SERVICES
1030 Massachusetts Ave.
Cambridge, MA 02138
800-695-4005

PRODIGY SERVICES
445 Hamilton Avenue
White Plains, NY 10601
800-776-3449

For Further Reading

The following is a list of a few of the current books that will make your entry into the Internet easier. New books and manuals about the Internet are constantly being published and can be found at most public libraries and book stores.

Internet: Getting Started, by April Marine
The On-Line Job Search Companion, by James C. Gonyea
The Internet Complete Reference, by Harley Hahn & Rick Stout
The Internet Yellow Pages, by Harley Hahn & Rick Stout
Using the Internet, by Mary Ann Pike
Guide to Information Access, by The American Library Association
Internet Basics: Your On-Line Access to the Global Electronic Superhighway, by Steve Lambert & Walter Howe
Be Your Own Headhunter — Go Online and Get the Job You Want, by Pam Dixon and Sylvia Tierston
Finding A Job on the Internet, by Allen Glossbrenner

Chapter 11

KEEPING RECORDS

Before you conclude your job hunt, you will have met many people, sent out dozens of resumes and letters and made countless telephone calls. You will have also given and received information on salaries, job specifications, qualifications, dates, telephone numbers, addresses, names, and titles.

In fact, enough information will flow through you to keep a small computer busy. Failure to keep accurate records of telephone conversations, interviews, resumes, and letters can get you into trouble and even cause you to lose a job opportunity.

Staying on Top of Your Campaign

Maintaining a systematic record file is most important when you are negotiating an offer with a prospective employer. It usually takes more than one interview to get hired and in some cases four or five different interviewers get into the act. First the personnel manager or an assistant, then the head of the department in which the job exists, and perhaps a divisional manager or a vice president. Then, back to the personnel department.

Everyone along the line will be evaluating you and making copious notes about every aspect of your education and background, running up a hefty dossier. You will never see this record, so if you don't keep your facts straight from one interviewer to another, you are bound to get into trouble somewhere along the line.

You can devise any record-keeping system that you are comfortable with and that does the job. One of the most efficient systems consists of setting up a standard manila file folder for every contact you make. Each folder can accommodate copies of letters you write and receive, plus folders, booklets, annual reports, and other information on each company with whom you are in contact.

In the folder you also can keep notes made at interviews, business cards, and all forms pertaining to the job and the firm.

By attaching a few lined 8½" x 11" sheets to each folder you can keep a running diary of all of your calls and meetings. This system permits you to stay on top of all of your activities, and provides you with instant recall of facts, names, addresses, telephone numbers, and figures when you most need them.

If you have ready access to a computer, you might prefer to create files in which you store copies of correspondence you send, records of persons with whom you spoke or met, and what transpired with each contact. Computer files are neat, compact, easily updated, and easy to refer to when needed. You will have to maintain supplementary paper files, however, in which to keep business cards and correspondence received.

Chapter 12

THE INTERVIEW

Hundreds of books and articles have been written on the subject of interviews, both from the viewpoint of the employer and the applicant. Industrial psychologists, psychiatrists, Harvard Business School professors, behavioral scientists, and self-styled experts of all persuasions have agonized over the interview and then brought forth voluminous texts. Covered in these books are stress interviews, patterned interviews, depth interviews, and all sorts of personalized interview techniques invented by individual personnel managers.

By whatever name it is called, an interview boils down to two basics: do you have the primary qualifications for the job—and does the interviewer like you. The latter consideration is often more important than the former. I have had many personnel managers tell me that an applicant's background, experience, and education were perfect for the job, but there was something that they didn't like about the individual. They could not pinpoint it, but for some reason the chemistry did not match. Unfortunately, interviewers do make value judgments based on first impressions. Consequently, the most qualified applicant does not always get the job.

Interviewing Methods Vary

Interviewing techniques differ from one personnel department to another. Some personnel people interview strictly "by the book." They use the latest methods devised by psychologists, sociologists, and human resources specialists. They conduct structured interviews working from an elaborate series of check lists and questions.

The stress interview, for example, is designed to put you completely on the defensive by throwing very intimate and seemingly irrelevant questions at you to get your reactions. This technique may take any number of forms. The interviewer, after seating you, simply says, "tell me about yourself," and he does not utter another word for the next 15 minutes. By letting you talk about yourself, you are given the opportunity to make an impressive case for yourself. It may seem like an easy way to talk your way into a job, but when faced with a long silence and a stony stare, you very often find yourself saying too much and ending up with your foot in your mouth.

Some interviewers who adhere to the stress principle use more obnoxious tactics, interrupting you frequently, asking personal questions about your finances, your family, and your sex life, looking at papers while you are talking, and other actions designed to disturb you. The idea behind this game is presumably to see how you handle an unexpected situation and to get your reactions. The proponents of this kind of interview justify its use by reasoning that if you crumble at this stage of the game, you would do the same under the daily pressures of the job—a rather weak theory at best. Stress interviews are used mostly to recruit executive personnel, but I have heard of them used on recent college graduates, many of whom I would surmise either head right back to the campus or beat a path to the nearest bar.

Many people think the stress interview is pure nonsense. They feel that you cannot evoke legitimate responses by asking irrelevant and impertinent questions which are not only embarrassing and demeaning, but often unanswerable.

The Informal or Conversational Interview

On the other hand, you may often meet an interviewer who really does not interview. He holds an informal discussion, the objective being to put you completely at ease, hoping to get a better glimpse of your background and personality without the structure of a formal question and answer session. These interviews often turn into a bull session with the applicant interviewing the interviewer. If you become involved in a session of this kind, you will probably come away with the feeling that you had a pleasant chat, but there remained a lot of unanswered questions.

It's no accident that the interviewer is cozying up to you and letting you open up. What usually happens is that you will be so relieved at the warmth and friendliness, that you will respond by being completely candid and, as a result, divulge information that, under more formal circumstances, you would not dare to admit.

Bernard C., one such victim of his own honesty, was a recent graduate of a highly rated eastern university. He held a BA in Finance and an MA in Economics, and was referred by me to an internationally known consulting firm for a job as a trainee in their research department. The personnel manager gave him the "old buddy" treatment, and, as it turned out, the interviewer and Bernard discovered they had gone to the same university. That was all that was needed. The interview turned into a nostalgic free-for-all, and when it was all over, the applicant had confessed to a number of improprieties plus the serious admission of an off-campus arrest. Bernard made the mistake of forgetting who he was talking to and why he was there. Completely disarmed by his "old buddy," the interviewer, he had destroyed his chance for the job.

You will probably be exposed at one time or another to both of these techniques. Most personnel managers, however, avoid either extreme and through the use of intelligent, experienced probing, make the interview a business-like, but pleasant experience from which both parties come away with knowledge of the other's needs and objectives.

Each interviewer varies in his approach. After a while you will become an expert in identifying the technique used and be able to adjust your responses accordingly.

Prepare or Perish

Regardless of the form it takes, you must be adequately prepared. This means that before you go into any interview, you should know as much as possible about the following:

The Specifications of the Job

The amount of information you can get depends upon where you heard about the position. If you are called into an interview on the basis of a small classified advertisement which you have answered, you won't know too much before the interview. Frequently you are not even made aware of the salary range being offered. However, if you were referred through an employment agency or a recruiter, you have the opportunity and advantage of getting—ahead of time—all of the information you will need.

But to get the information you have to ask for it. Unfortunately, too many employment agency people fail to get all the important facts about a job—or, if they do have them, they are too lazy or do not care enough to pass them on to you. Do not hesitate to insist on full disclosure of the job specifications. If the counselor does not have them, ask that he contact his client and get the details. You are entitled to them, and you will have a better chance at the job if you have them. A major reason for going to an employment agency is to gain the advantage of having all of the facts about a job. Equipped with them, you can go fully prepared for an interview.

Information About the Company

If you have never heard of the company, try to find out all you can about it. How large is it? How long has it been in business? If it is a manufacturer, how many plants does it have and where are they located? How many employees do they have? What is the volume of business? What type of customers does it serve (industrial, trade, or consumer)? Is its business local, national, or worldwide? Who is the president? What is the name of the manager of the department the prospective opening is in?

If you cannot get this information from the agency or other contacts, there are sources readily available to you. Refer to the list of directories and publications on pages 159–171. Most of them offer complete breakdowns of personnel and operational facts.

Comprehensive financial information about any publicly owned corporation (one whose stock is traded on an exchange) can be obtained by writing to the controller or treasurer and requesting a copy of their Form 10-K. This is a financial disclosure form which, by law, must be filed with the Securities and Exchange Commission and sent to anyone who requests it. A copy of the company's annual report can be obtained from the same source or from any stockbroker.

Information on privately held companies can be obtained from your local Chamber of Commerce or State Industrial Development Agency.

With all of the sources listed above plus the directories shown in Appendix 5 there is no excuse for anyone to walk into an interview without a good knowledge of the company.

The reason for all of this preparation should be obvious. You will be in a better position to ask intelligent questions about your place in the firm. You will also impress your interviewer with your knowledge of his company. A personnel manager will often ask "What do you know about our company?" If your response is a blank stare, you are off to a bad start. You do not have to know everything about a company, but even a little knowledge will help your cause.

Having sufficient information about a firm will also enable you to talk in terms of what you can do for them. Your interviewer, through your resume, knows what you have done for other companies, but his main concern is what you can do for his company. Without at least a basic knowledge of the firm's structure and operations and the specifics of the job opening, you are hardly in a position to intelligently handle this important aspect.

Have Your Answers Ready

Here are some of the questions you can expect to be asked in an interview. Study this list and jot down on a piece of paper what your answers would be.

(1)   What do you think you can contribute to our company?
(2)   What are your strengths and weaknesses?
(3)   What are your career goals?
(4)   What are your objectives? Immediate and future?
(5)   What satisfactions do you get from a job?
(6)   What kind of a manager do you think you would make?
(7)   Do you work well under pressure?

(8)   What would you consider your highest achievement in the past 2 years?

(9)   Are you satisfied with your present salary level?

(10)   What is your minimum salary requirement at this time?

(11)   Have you ever fired anyone yourself? Did you find it difficult?

(12)   What other jobs are you considering?

(13)   What kind of a position would you like to be in 10 years from now?

(14)   Do you intend to continue your education?

(15)   Can you make quick decisions?

(16)   If you made a decision that turned out to be wrong, how would you handle the situation?

(17)   How would you describe your personality?

(18)   Why did you leave your last job?

(19)   Are you ill at ease in a group of people you have just met?

(20)   What are your hobbies?

(21)   What do you rate higher in a job, challenge or stability?

(22)   What is your opinion of your last employer?

(23)   By what criteria do you judge an employee's performance?

(24)   Why are you looking for a change in employment?

Personal Appearance

Poor personal appearance is frequently at the head of the list of negative factors that lead to a rejection of a job applicant. Getting turned down because you don't have the qualifications for a position or have less experience than another candidate is not your fault. But you will have only yourself to blame if you get written off because of your appearance and dress.

First impressions are crucial. You can lose the job during the first five minutes of an interview. Different types of firms have different dress codes, but don't try to guess what they are for the interview. After you're hired you can adjust your wardrobe accordingly. As a general rule, be traditional rather than trendy. Dress conservatively for your first interview.

Enthusiasm—The Extra Ingredient

Ralph Waldo Emerson wasn't looking for a job when he said: "Nothing great was ever achieved without enthusiasm," but he spoke the truth.

Enthusiasm is a great weight in the balance. When your competitor has an extra university degree and two more years of experience, enthusiasm can tip the scales in your favor.

If you are not sure whether you are interested in the position or the company, act as if you are. Make your interviewer believe that he or she is offering a terrific opportunity. Leave every interviewer with the best impression you can, even if you are completely disinterested in the job. Executives tend to remember the interested and enthusiastic applicant and they may be in a position to recommend you to another department at a later time.

Visual Aids

Certain occupations require visible credentials. The obvious ones are advertising, art, and communications. Interviewers report that people seeking jobs in these areas appear without portfolios, hoping to convince them that they are qualified without bringing supporting evidence.

Even if you are a beginner in any one of these areas, you should show samples of your work. They can be school samples or unpublished material, but bring *something*. You won't get to first base without it. Samples of your work will be helpful in occupations other than creative. Market researchers, financial analysts and salespeople all appreciate visual aids. Reports, sales performance records, marketing studies, proposals, and presentations—these are all evidence of your capabilities and should be shown at an interview.

If you were given any citations, awards or prizes or had anything published either in school or on the job, bring them to the interview. Letters of recommendation from former employers are also valuable. As I mentioned before, it's a good policy to get a reference letter when you leave a job. It prevents any problems with references at a later time.

Tips for the Interview

(1) Don't mumble. Open your mouth and speak clearly.

(2) Use the interviewer's name often during the session. It helps maintain a friendly atmosphere.

(3) Offer your hand upon coming into the office—whether or not your interviewer does so first. Grasp the hand firmly. A handful of rubber fingers and a limp wrist do not engender confidence.

(4) Smile frequently, but not continuously. Halloween pumpkins are out of season.

(5) Inject enthusiasm into your conversation. Act as if you're really glad to be there (even though you would rather be at the movies). Avoid going on in a singsong voice. Your interviewer probably would rather be at the movies too, so try to keep him or her awake.

(6) Treat the outer office staff the same way you would treat your interviewer. The receptionist and secretary might be asked for their opinion of you later.

(7) If you are asked to fill out an application before the interview, do it without complaint or comments such as "I have a resume," or "I would rather speak to Ms. Jones first" or "I don't have time for such nonsense." Fill out the form completely. Don't write "see resume" as a substitute. Your ability to follow instructions is a part of the interview process. If you detect any question on the application form that you deem to be too personal, leave it blank and discuss it with your interviewer.

(8) Do not schedule more than two interviews a day—one in the morning and one in the afternoon. You cannot judge whether an interview will take one hour or three. You will have enough pressure on you without having to worry about the time.

(9) Restrict your questions to those concerning the job. Don't ask about vacations or benefits at the initial interview.

(10) Don't try to entertain your interviewer. A little humor is OK but don't be a clown.

(11) Don't judge the entire company by the questions or attitude of the person interviewing you. (He or she may seem to be unsympathetic or unreasonably rough, but this can be a way of getting at the facts.)

(12) Don't smoke even if your interviewer does and invites you to join him or her—unless you are being interviewed for a job with a tobacco company.

(13) Never criticize a former employer, school instructor or anyone with whom you were associated. It's bad form and puts your interviewer on notice that you might have difficulty getting along with people.

(14) Don't be a name dropper. Telling your interviewer that you belong to the same country club as Jim Fergusen, the operations vice-president, or that your father was in the same fraternity with the chairman of the board, will not impress him one bit. It may have the opposite effect. Such statements are often perceived as slightly intimidating. It's like telling a cop who is giving you a ticket that you have friends at headquarters.

(15) Be confident. The firm is as much in need of your services as you are in need of a job. Don't try too hard. Avoid giving the impression that you are desperate for a job, and that you will do anything to get one. Showing some independence is good. This is not easy to do when you have been out of work for a while, but any anxiety that comes across to your interviewer can have a negative effect.

(16) When the interview is over, don't linger, or use the last few moments to attempt to flatter the interviewer or the company. Simply say something like: "If I can provide any further information, I hope you will contact me," or "Thank you very much for your time. I hope I will be hearing from you soon." Then leave. For better or worse, it's over.

Chapter 13

AFTER THE INTERVIEW

If you have prepared yourself properly before the interview and conducted yourself well during it, what further steps can you take to help your chances? There is one at this point that is so effective and simple that it is surprising that it is done so infrequently.

If you are really interested in the position, as soon as you get home or back to your office after your interview, sit down and write a note to your interviewer, thanking him for his time. This small courtesy can work miracles. I have seen many situations in which employers who were undecided about an applicant suddenly become enthusiastic after receiving such a note. It may not be the deciding factor, but it can give you a couple of points on your competition.

Do not underestimate this seemingly insignificant action. Personnel people interview all day. They are continually in an adversary position with job applicants, trying to ferret out information which is sometimes reluctantly given, being pleasant when they do not feel like it. The boredom of the daily routine can jade even the most equable person. The receipt of a thank-you note becomes a major event, simply because it is such a rare occurrence. The applicant who takes the time to send a note may be well rewarded.

Keep It Short

The follow-up letter should be short, and contain the following statements:

(1) You appreciate the interview time.
(2) You are sure of your ability to do the job.
(3) Call attention to the most important aspect of the position and express your confidence in your ability to handle it.
(4) You hope that you are being considered for the job.

Do not write a long letter in an attempt to sell yourself, or rehash the interview. This would only defeat the purpose of the note. Sample letters of this type appear on pages 143 and 144.

Review and Analyze Your Performance

Make each interview a learning experience. To improve your technique for future interviews, complete the forms on pages 144–146 and file a copy in the appropriate prospect folder.

Interview Summary

This form should be completed after each interview and retained in your prospect file. Enter your impressions of the job, your interviewer, and the company. Record all information about salary, benefits, and other pertinent data. Then complete the analysis form.

Company _____

Address _____ Telephone _____

Interviewer and title _____

Product or service _____

Position _____ Salary _____

Source _____
                    (Advertisement, direct contact, personal, etc)

Description of duties and responsibilities _____

_____

_____

_____

_____

General interview notes _____
                              (Impression of position and company)

_____

_____

_____

_____

Salary negotiations, fringe benefits, etc _____

_____

_____

Results of interview _____

_____

Follow-up _____
                      (Letters and calls—dates and results)

_____

Interview Analysis

Try to recall what questions were asked and how you responded to them. It is painful to recall situations which you feel you handled badly, but if your replies to any of the following questions are negative, write down the points to be clarified in subsequent mail, telephone or personal contacts with this particular company.

_____

Did I forget to mention anything about my background that would have helped me?

_____

_____

Did I come on too strong? Not strong enough? _____

_____

_____

Do I have all the information I need about the job? _____

_____

_____

Did I neglect to ask the right questions? What, if anything, did I leave out? _____

_____

_____

Am I clear on the duties and responsibilities of the job? _____

_____

_____

Where did I make the biggest mistake during the interview? _____

_____

_____

Where did I appear to make the most favorable impression? _____

_____

_____

Did I talk too much? Too little? _____

_____

_____

Did I answer all questions clearly? _____

_____

_____

Did I make any gaffes in statements, gestures, questions or answers? _____

_____

_____

Were they serious, or am I overestimating their importance? _____

_____

_____

Did I make a good presentation? Was I properly dressed? _____

_____

_____

Did I handle the salary discussion properly? _____

_____

_____

Do I know all there is to know about the fringe benefit package? _____

_____

_____

Sample Interview Follow-up Letters

Laura Anderson
2416 West 8th Street
Philadelphia, PA 19156

February 18, 19--

Mr. George Gilliam
Employment Manager
National Food Corp.
325 Main Street
Ardmore, PA 16902

Dear Mr. Gilliam:

This is to express my appreciation for your courtesy in granting me an interview yesterday for the position of Payroll Manager.

I am very interested in this position, and feel confident that my training and experience will enable me to competently perform the duties which you described. I feel particularly qualified to handle the supervisory aspect of the job.

Your interest and consideration are greatly appreciated, and I look forward to hearing from you further.

Sincerely yours,

Laura Anderson

JACK HENNING
425 S.W. 8th Avenue
Miami, FL   33143

305-555-9834

April 13, 19-

Mr. Mark Strassing
Claims Manager
Southeastern Insurance Co.
1235 Dade Boulevard
Miami, FL 33165

Dear Mr. Strassing:

   Thank you very much for the opportunity
to speak with you regarding the position
with your organization.

   From what you described about the duties
and responsibilities of the position, I feel
certain that I can perform them efficiently.
As I mentioned during the interview I have
been closely involved in the investigation
and reporting of automobile property and
liability claims for the past four years.
Your position seems to offer both the challenge
and the opportunity that I have been looking
for.

   I will be happy to supply any further
information you might require and I appreciate
your interest and consideration.

                              Sincerely,

                              JACK HENNING

Chapter 14
IN CONCLUSION

There is a job for you out there. It may take you longer to find it than you anticipated, but the fact that you have read this book indicates that you are serious enough about your job search to seek advice.

Your greatest problem is not your competition, or the job market, or the economy. It is your own attitude. If, when things seem to go from bad to worse and everything seems to turn out the wrong way, you allow yourself to become discouraged, you will really be in trouble. It is almost impossible to hide despair, and a discouraged, demoralized job hunter carries it around with him like a ball and chain. Employers sense it and it makes them uncomfortable.

More important, it affects your personality. I almost always know when an applicant is having a real tough time getting a job. There is no stereotype for despair, but there is a quality which tells me that here is a person who is losing confidence.

Getting discouraged is one thing. Anyone looking for a job, with all its problems and frustrations, is entitled to low periods. But letting the discouragement overwhelm you so much that you cannot function properly does serious damage to your job campaign. If you do all the things you should, and spend all the time you should in your search, you will have no time for discouragement—and you will find the job you want.

Final Thank You Letters

After you have successfully completed your job hunt and are happily employed, there is one more step to be taken—and one which, unfortunately, very few people do. It only takes a little time and effort, but it is well worth the investment. Write a note to those individuals whom you felt have sincerely tried to help you or who have shown some concern or kindness along the way. Send it to personnel managers who have interviewed you, friends who have commiserated with you and especially employment agencies who have made an effort on your behalf (without compensation, incidentally). It is not only the right thing to do. You may be in a position again where you will need their services and help.

Your thoughtfulness in remembering them may bear fruit at some time in the future. Following this chapter are some sample "thank you" letters and I recommend strongly that you send them out to your list of contacts.

Study the bibliography at the end of the book for sources of further information. There are many excellent books and periodicals on the subject of jobs and careers and you owe it to yourself to make every effort to get as much information on the subject as possible.

Good luck!

Sample Thank You Letters

John K. Hurley
116 Washington St.
Philadelphia, Pa. 19146

(215) 555-8694

Mr. Jack Broward
Broward-Manley Personnel Agency
1215 Chestnut Street
Philadelphia, Pa. 19253

Dear Jack:

    I am happy to report that I have accepted
a position with the Warington Pump Company as
an Office Services Manager.

    I know that my diversified background made
me a difficult candidate for a career placement
professional like yourself to sell. I especially
want to thank you for your moral support and
special effort in my behalf.

    If I can be of any service to you, please
feel free to contact me.

                            Sincerely,

BERNICE JONES
428 Main Street
Chicago, IL 60063

April 28, 19--

Mr. Richard Serino
National Sales Managers Association
1400 Madison Street
Chicago, IL   60234

Dear Mr. Serino:

The advice and guidance I received from your organization were invaluable in helping me to obtain my present new position with the Midcontinent Surety Corporation. I am particularly grateful for the helpful hints provided through the meetings of your Resume Clinic.

Not only did I get more interviews by using the methods recommended by your placement committee, but the courtesy and understanding shown by your entire staff gave me a much needed lift during a particularly difficult time.

If I can be of any service to you or your organization at any time, please do not hesitate to contact me.

Cordially,

Douglas Cook
223 E. Dauphin Ave.
Philadelphia, PA 19122
April 23, 19--

Ms. Nancy Spring
CF Industries, Inc.
324 Chestnut St.
Philadelphia, PA 19119

Dear Nancy:

My new job with Blue Lake Chemical Company starts next Monday, and your very generous recommendation was instrumental in my receiving the offer.

As you know, it was your letter of introduction that got me the interview, and your subsequent follow-up clinched it for me.

For that you have my sincere gratitude.

Cordially,

142 Henry Street
Port Chester, New York 10134
September 13, 19--

Mr. Albert Davis
Consolidated Personnel Agency
437 Fifth Avenue
New York, NY 10017

Dear Mr. Davis:

I am happy to inform you that my job search for a position as Advertising Manager has ended. I have just accepted such a position with a national manufacturing company in Westchester.

I feel that I have been very fortunate to have been able to choose from a number of job offers during such a tight labor market. This has been due to the extended efforts that you and a few other agencies have given to me. I am deeply grateful for your services.

Sincerely,

Catherine Foley

APPENDIX 1

JOB SEARCH CONTROL SHEET

Record all correspondence, applications, networking contacts, and interviews to provide a quick picture of your daily activities.

DATE	NAME OF COMPANY AND INDIVIDUAL	TYPE OF CONTACT Letter, personal meeting, referral, etc.	DATE OF FOLLOW-UP	STATUS OF CONTACT Replies, interviews, etc.

APPENDIX 2—TEST YOUR SUCCESS FACTORS

On the following chart, check the boxes which you believe represent your strengths in each of the qualities listed. They are all positive attributes that would contribute to success in any career.

If you have been completely honest in your scoring, a quick analysis of the completed chart will reveal your strengths and weaknesses.

		Very	Moderately	Not Very	Not at all
AGGRESSIVE:	Outgoing—forceful				
AMBITIOUS:	Career-oriented—strong desire to attain personal and financial success				
ANALYTICAL:	Good problem solver—logical mind				
ARTICULATE:	Able to communicate ideas and opinions clearly and forcefully				
ASSERTIVE:	Not afraid to give opinions or make suggestions				
CHEERFUL:	Pleasant demeanor—able to smile easily				
COMPETITIVE:	Intense desire to win				
CONFIDENT:	High level of self-esteem—self-assured				
CONSCIENTIOUS:	Good work habits—able to take on unpleasant tasks—punctual				
COOPERATIVE:	Helpful—good team worker				
CREATIVE:	Innovative—able to improve on ideas and produce new concepts				
DEPENDABLE:	Steady—keep promises—good work habits				
EFFICIENT:	Make good use of time—high quality work performance				

157

		Very	Moderately	Not Very	Not at all
ENERGETIC:	High level of mental and physical endurance—work quickly				
ENTHUSIASTIC:	Interested—eager to accomplish tasks—lively in manner and speech				
FRIENDLY:	Congenial in relationships with associates and strangers				
INDUSTRIOUS:	Hard-working—eager to take on difficult tasks				
LOGICAL:	Able to assimilate information, analyze difficult problems, and arrive at viable solutions				
LOYAL:	Supportive of the best interests of company and colleagues				
OPTIMISTIC:	Hopeful—expectant—convinced that everything will turn out well				
ORGANIZED:	Orderly—efficient planner				
PERSEVERING:	Undaunted by setbacks—determined to see a job through even under difficult circumstances				
POISED:	Maintain dignified, calm demeanor regardless of provocation or pressure				
PRECISE:	High standard of perfection in all activities				
SELF-CONTROLLED:	Slow to anger—keep your head in tense situations				
SINCERE:	Caring—in personal and professional relationships				
TACTFUL:	Able to deal with opposing opinions and actions without rancor				
UNDERSTANDING:	Sympathetic—tolerant				

APPENDIX 3—SOURCES OF INFORMATION BY OCCUPATION

Accounting

Directories
Business and Finance Career Directory
Gale Research, Inc.
835 Penobscot Bldg.
Detroit, MI 48226

Kohlers Directory of Accountants
Prentice-Hall Publishing Co.
Englewood Cliffs, NJ 07632

Periodicals
Journal of Accountancy of CPAs
Harborside Financial Center
201 Plaza 3
Jersey City, NJ 07311

National Public Accountant
1010 N. Fairfax St.
Alexandria, VA 22314

Organizations
American Institute of Certified Public
Accountants
1211 Avenue of the Americas
New York, NY 10036

National Society of Public Accountants
1010 N. Fairfax St.
Alexandria, VA 22314

Financial Executives Institute
10 Madison Ave.
Morristown, NJ 07960

Administration

Directories
*Standard & Poors Register of
Corporations, Directors & Executives*
25 Broadway
New York, NY 10004

Periodicals
Across the Board
The Conference Board
845 Third Ave.
New York, NY 10022

Boardroom Reports
55 Railroad Avenue
Greenwich, CT 06836

Organizations
Society for Administrative Management
126 Lee Ave.
Vinton, VA 24179

American Management Association
135 W. 50th St.
New York, NY 10020

Advertising

Directories
Madison Avenue Handbook
42 W. 38th St.
New York, NY 10018

Standard Directory of Advertisers
National Register Publishing Co.
121 Chanlon Road
New Providence, NJ 07974

Periodicals
Advertising Age
220 E. 42nd St.
New York, NY 10017

Journal of Advertising Research
641 Lexington Ave.
New York, NY 10022

Organizations
Advertising Council
261 Madison Avenue
New York, NY 10016

Architecture

Directories
Accredited Programs for Architecture
1735 New York Ave., NW
Washington, DC 20006

Periodicals
Architectural Record
1221 Avenue of the Americas
New York, NY 10020

Progressive Architecture
620 Summer St.
Stamford, CT 06904

Organizations
American Institute of Architects
1735 New York Ave., NW
Washington, DC 20006

Audio/Visual

Directories
Video Source Book
Gale Research, Inc.
835 Penobscot Bldg.
Detroit, MI 48226

Periodicals
*Advertising Presentations Development
and Delivery*
445 Broad Hollow Rd.
Melville, NY 11747

Audio-Visual International Magazine
275 Madison Ave.
New York, NY 10016

Organizations
Audio-Visual Management Association
665 Mokena Drive
Miami Springs, FL 33166

Banking

Directories
American Bank Directory
McFadden Business Publications
6195 Crooked Creek Rd.
Norcross, GA 30092

*Directory of American Savings & Loan
Associations*
1115 E. 30th St.
Baltimore, MD 21218

Periodicals
American Banker — Bond Buyer
1 State Street Plaza
New York, NY 10004

Organizations
American Bankers Association
1120 Connecticut Ave., NW
Washington, DC 20036

Consumer Bankers Association
100 Wilson Blvd.
Arlington, VA 22209

Civil Engineering

Directories
ASCE Directory — Official Register
American Society of Civil Engineers
345 E. 47th St.
New York, NY 10017

ENR Directory of Contractors
1221 Avenue of the Americas
New York, NY 10020

Periodicals
Civil Engineering Magazine
345 E. 47th St.
New York, NY 10017

Construction Products
Cahners Publishing
1350 E. Touhy Ave.
Des Plains, IA 60017

Organizations
American Society of Civil Engineers
347 E. 47th St.
New York, NY 10017

Commercial Art

Directories
*Artists Market — Where to Sell Your
Artwork*
F & W Publications
1507 Dana Ave.
Cincinnati, OH 45207

Graphic Arts Blue Book
A.F. Lewis & Co.
79 Madison Ave.
New York, NY 10016

Periodicals
Art Direction
Advertising Trade Publications
10 E. 39th St.
New York, NY 10016

Organizations
Art Directors Club
250 Park Avenue South
New York, NY 10003

Communications

Directories
World Book of IABC
International Association of Business
Communicators
One Hallidie Plaza
San Francisco, CA 94102

*O'Dwyers Directory of Corporate
Communications Executives*
271 Madison Ave.
New York, NY 10016

Periodicals
Journal of Business Communications
College of Business Administration
University of North Texas
Denton, TX 76203

Organizations
International Association of Business
Communicators
One Hallidie Plaza
San Francisco, CA 94102

Society for Technical Communications
901 Stuart St.
Arlington, VA 22203

Computers

Directories
Computer Review
594 Marrett Rd.
Lexington, MA 02173

Data Communications Buyers Guide
1221 Avenue of the Americas
New York, NY 10020

Periodicals
Communications Week
600 Community Drive
Manhasset, NY 11031

Online
462 Danbury Rd.
Wilton, CT 06897

Organizations
Association of Data Communications
Users
P.O. Box 385728
Bloomington, MN 55438

Computer and Communications
Industry Association
666 11th St., NW
Washington, DC 20001

Consultants

Directories
Directory of Management Consultants
Kennedy Publications
Templeton Road
Fitzwilliam, NH 03447

Dun's Consultants Directory
Dun & Bradstreet Information Services
3 Sylvan Way
Parsippany, NJ 07054

Periodicals
Consultant's News
Kennedy Publications
Templeton Road
Fitzwilliam, NH 03447

Organizations
Council of Consulting Organizations
521 Fifth Ave.
New York, NY 10175

Credit

Periodicals
Credit Magazine
1101 14th St., NW
Washington, DC 20005

Organizations
National Association of Credit
Management
8815 Centre Park Dr.
Columbia, MD 21045

National Institute of Credit
8815 Centre Park Dr.
Columbia, MD 21045

Economics

Periodicals
American Economic Review
2014 Broadway
Nashville, TN 37203

Journal of Economics & Business
Elsevier Science Publishing Co.
Madison Square Station
P.O. Box 882
New York, NY 10159

Organizations
National Association of Business
Economists
28790 Chagrin Blvd.
Cleveland, OH 33122

Electronics

Directories
Electronic Industry Telephone Directory
Harris Publishing Co.
2057 Aurora Rd.
Twinsburg, OH 44087

Periodicals
Electronic Business
275 Washington St.
Newton, MA 02158

Electronic Design
Cahners Publishing Co.
2025 Gateway Place
San Jose, CA 95110

Organizations
American Electronics Assn.
5201 Great American Pkwy
Santa Clara, CA 95054

Electronic Industries Assn.
2001 Pennsylvania Avenue
Washington, DC 20006

Fashion

Directories
Fairchild Dictionary of Fashion
Fairchild Books
7 W. 34th St.
New York, NY 10001

Periodicals
DNR
Fashion & Merchandising Group
7 W. 34th St.
New York, NY 10001

Gentlemens Quarterly/GQ
Conde Nast Publications
350 Madison Ave.
New York, NY 10017

Womens Wear Daily
Fairchild Books
7 W. 34th St.
New York, NY 10001

Organizations
Council of Fashion Designers of
America
1412 Broadway
New York, NY 10018

Men's Fashion Association of America
475 Park Avenue South
New York, NY 10016

Finance

Directories
*Directory of Business and Financial
Services*
Special Libraries Assn.
1700 18th St., NW
Washington, DC 20009

Periodicals
Commercial & Financial Chronicle
P.O. Box 1839
Daytona Beach, FL 32115

Journal of Financial Economics
P.O. Box 822
Madison Square Station
New York, NY 10159

Financial World
1328 Broadway
New York, NY 10001

Organizations
Financial Executives Institute
10 Madison Ave.
Morristown, NJ 07960

American Financial Services Assn.
919 18th St., NW
Washington, DC 20006

Graphic Arts

Directories
Graphic Arts Monthly
249 W. 17th St.
New York, NY 10021

Inplant Reproductions
North American Publishing Co.
401 Broad St.
Philadelphia, PA 19108

Organizations
American Institute of Graphic Arts
1059 Third Ave.
New York, NY 10021

Society of American Graphic Artists
21 Union Square
New York, NY 10003

Health Care

Directories
AHA Guide to the Health Care Field
840 N. Lake Shore Dr.
Chicago, IL 60611

Health Care Career Directory
Gale Research, Inc.
835 Penobscot Bldg.
Detroit, MI 48026

Periodicals
American Journal of Nursing
555 W. 57th St.
New York, NY 10019

Health Business
1133 15th St., NW
Washington, DC 20005

Health Care Executive
840 N. Lake Shore Dr.
Chicago, IL 60611

Organizations
American Academy of Medical
Administrators
30555 Southfield Rd.
Southfield, MI 48076

American Hospital Association
840 N. Lake Shore Dr.
Chicago, IL 60611

Insurance

Directories
Hine's Directory of Insurance Adjustors
P.O. Box 280
Glen Ellyn, IL 60138

Periodicals
Insurance Market
The Rough Notes Co.
1200 Meridian St.
Indianapolis, IN 46206

Insurance Advocate
P.O. Box 9001
Mt. Vernon, NY 10552

Insurance Week
1001 Fourth Ave.
Seattle, WA 98154

Organizations
Insurance Services Office
7 World Trade Center
New York, NY 10048

National Insurance Assn.
P.O. Box 53230
Chicago, IL 60653

Risk and Management Society
205 E. 42nd St.
New York, NY 10017

Journalism

Directories
Journalism Career & Scholarship Guide
Dow Jones Newspaper Fund, Inc.
P.O. Box 300
Princeton, NJ 08543

Periodicals
Columbia Journalism Review
Columbia University
700 Journalism Bldg.
New York, NY 10027

Editor & Publisher
11 W. 19th St.
New York, NY 10011

Organizations
Society of Professional Journalists
Sigma Delta Chi
16 Jackson St.
Greencastle, IN 46135

Law

Directories
Law & Legal Information Directory
Gale Research, Inc.
835 Penobscot Bldg.
Detroit, MI 48226

Guide to American Law
West Publishing
P.O. Box 64526
St. Paul, MN 55164

Periodicals
Legal Times
1730 M St., NW
Washington, DC 20036

National Law Journal
111 Eighth Ave.
New York, NY 10011

Organizations
American Bar Association
750 N. Lake Shore Dr.
Chicago, IL 60611

Library Science

Directories
American Library Directory
121 Chanlon Rd.
New Providence, NJ 07974

Periodicals
American Libraries
50 E. Huron St.
Chicago, IL 60611

Library Journal
249 W. 17th St.
New York, NY 10011

Wilson Library Bulletin
950 University Place
Bronx, NY 10452

Organizations
Special Libraries Assn.
1700 18th St., NW
Washington, DC 20009

Marketing

Directories
Marketing & Sales Career Directory
835 Penobscot Bldg.
Detroit, MI 48226

Incentive
Bill Communications
355 Park Avenue South
New York, NY 10010

Journal of Marketing Research
250 S. Wacker Dr.
Chicago, IL 60606

Sales & Marketing Management
Bill Communications
355 Park Avenue South
New York, NY 10010

Organizations
American Marketing Assn.
250 S. Wacker Drive
Chicago, IL 60606

Sales & Marketing Executives, Intl.
Statler Office Tower
Cleveland, OH 44115

Personnel

Directories
Personnel Executives Contact Book
835 Penobscot Bldg.
Detroit, MI 48226

Periodicals
Personnel Journal
P.O. Box 2440
Costa Mesa, CA 92628

H.R. Magazine
Society of Human Resource
Management
606 N. Washington St.
Alexandria, VA 22314

Organizations
International Association for Personnel
Women
P.O. Box 969
Andover, MA 01810

Society of Human Resource
Management
606 N. Washington St.
Alexandria, VA 22314

Photography

Directories
*Membership Directory of the American
Society of Photographers*
P.O. Box 3191
Spartanburg, SC 29324

Photographers Marketing Guide
1507 Dana Ave.
Cincinnati, OH 45207

Periodicals
Industrial Photography
445 N. Hollow Rd.
Melville, NY 11747

Professional Photography
1090 Executive Way
Des Plaines, IL 60018

Organizations
American Society of Magazine
Photographers
419 Park Avenue South
New York, NY 10016

Professional Photographers of America
1090 Executive Way
Des Plaines, IL 60018

Public Relations

Directories
*O'Dwyer's Directory of Public Relations
Firms*
271 Madison Ave.
New York, NY 10016

Public Relations Journal Register Issue
Public Relations Society of America
33 Irving Place
New York, NY 10003

Periodicals
Public Relations Review
P.O. Box 1678
Greenwich, CT 06836

Organizations
Public Relations Society of America
33 Irving Place
New York, NY 10003

Publishing

Directories
Literary Market Place
121 Chanlon Rd.
New Providence, NJ 07974

American Book Trade Directory
121 Chanlon Rd.
New Providence, NJ 07974

Periodicals
Booklist
American Library Assn.
50 E. Huron St.
Chicago, IL 60611

Publishers Weekly
249 W. 17th St.
New York, NY 10011

Organizations
Association of American Publishers
71 Fifth Ave.
New York, NY 10003

Purchasing

Directories
Macrae's Blue Book
817 Broadway
New York, NY 10003

Thomas Register of American Manufacturers
Five Penn Plaza
New York, NY 10001

Periodicals
Industrial Purchasing Agent
Publications for Industry
21 Russell Woods Rd.
Great Neck, NY 11021

Telecommunications

Directories
Telecommunications Directory
Gale Research, Inc.
835 Penobscot Bldg.
Detroit, MI 48226

Periodicals
Communications News
1575 Eye St., NW
Washington, DC 20005

Telecommunications Week
817 Broadway
New York, NY 10003

Organizations
Telecommunications Association
858 S. Oak Park Rd.
Covina, CA 92705

Travel and Tourism

Directories
Travel Weekly's World Travel Directory
500 Plaza Dr.
Secaucus, NJ 07096

Periodicals
Travel Agent Magazine
801 Second Ave.
New York, NY 10017

Travel Trade
15 W. 44th St.
New York, NY 10036

Travel Weekly
500 Plaza Dr.
Secaucus, NJ 07096

Organizations
American Society of Travel Agents
1101 King St.
Alexandria, VA 22314

Travel Industry Association of America
1133 21st St., NW
Washington, DC 20036

Writing & Editing

Directories
Book Publishing Career Directory
Gale Research, Inc.
835 Penobscot Bldg.
Detroit, MI 48226

Literary Market Place (LMP)
R.R. Bowker Co.
121 Chanlon Rd.
New Providence, NJ 07974

Working Press of the Nation
121 Chanlon Rd.
New Providence, NJ 07974

Writer's Market
1507 Dana Ave.
Cincinnati, OH 45207

Writer's Handbook
The Writer, Inc.
120 Boylston St.
Boston, MA 02116

Periodicals
Publishers Weekly
249 W. 17th St.
New York, NY 10011

Writer's Digest
1507 Dana Ave.
Cincinnati, OH 45207

The Writer
120 Boylston St.
Boston, MA 02116

American Society of Journalists &
Authors
1501 Broadway
New York, NY 10036

Authors Guild
330 W. 42nd St.
New York, NY 10036

Organizations
American Society of Business Press
Editors
4445 Gilmer Lane
Cleveland, OH 44143

American Society of Magazine Editors
575 Lexington Ave.
New York, NY 10022

American Society of Newspaper Editors
P.O. Box 17004
Washington, DC 20041

APPENDIX 4—BUSINESS AND FINANCIAL PERIODICALS

Barron's
200 Liberty St.
New York, NY 10281

Boardroom Reports
55 Railroad Ave.
Greenwich, CT 06836

Crain Communications
  Crain's New York Business
  Crain's Chicago Business
  Crain's Cleveland Business
  Crain's Detroit Business
220 E. 42nd St.
New York, NY 10017

Financial World
1328 Broadway
New York, NY 10001

Forbes Magazine
60 Fifth Ave.
New York, NY 10011

Fortune Magazine
1271 Avenue of the Americas
New York, NY 10020

Inc. Magazine
488 Madison Ave.
New York, NY 10022

Institutional Investor
488 Madison Ave.
New York, NY 10022

Kiplinger's Personal Finance Magazine
Editors Park,
Maryland 20782

Money Magazine
1261 Avenue of the Americas
New York, NY 10020

Wall Street Journal
200 Liberty St.
New York, NY 10281

APPENDIX 5—LIST OF GENERAL SOURCE DIRECTORIES FOR JOB HUNTERS

The following directories are available in the reference section of most public libraries

COLLEGE PLACEMENT ANNUAL

DIRECTORY OF CORPORATE AFFILIATIONS

DIRECTORY OF EXECUTIVE RECRUITERS

DUN & BRADSTREET REFERENCE BOOK OF CORPORATE MANAGEMENT

DUN'S REGIONAL BUSINESS DIRECTORY

ENCYCLOPEDIA OF BUSINESS INFORMATION SOURCES

ENCYCLOPEDIA OF NON-PROFIT ASSOCIATIONS

FORTUNE DOUBLE 500 DIRECTORY

INC MAGAZINE DIRECTORY OF 500 FASTEST GROWING CORPORATIONS

JOB HUNTER'S GUIDE TO GREAT AMERICAN CITIES

MILLION DOLLAR DIRECTORY

MOODY'S INDUSTRIAL DIRECTORY

SRDS MEDIA DIRECTORIES

STANDARD & POOR'S REGISTER OF CORPORATIONS

STANDARD & POOR'S REGISTER OF DIRECTORS AND EXECUTIVES

STANDARD DIRECTORY OF ADVERTISING AGENCIES

STANDARD PERIODICAL DIRECTORY

STATE INDUSTRIAL DIRECTORIES (Published for all 50 states)

THE NATIONAL JOB BANK — GUIDE TO MAJOR U.S. EMPLOYERS

U.S. INDUSTRIAL DIRECTORY

(Information can also be obtained from local Chambers of Commerce or State Industrial Development Agencies)

APPENDIX 6—SUGGESTED FURTHER READING

Bird, Carolyn. *Second Careers — New Ways to Work After 50.* Boston, MA: Little Brown & Co. 1955.

Bolles, Richard N. *What Color is Your Parachute?* Berkeley, CA: Ten Speed Press, 1995.

Brandt, Ed with Leonard Corwen. *50 and Fired — How to Prepare For It — What To Do When It Happens.* Bedford, MA: Mills & Sanderson Publishers, 1988.

Corwen, Leonard. *College Not Required.* New York, NY: Macmillan General Reference, 1995.

————. *Successful Job Hunting.* Charleston, WV: Cambridge Educational, 1995.

DeLucca, Matthew J. *How to Get the Job You Want in 90 Days or Less.* New York: McGraw-Hill Book Co., 1994.

Drozdyk, Charlie. *Hot Jobs.* New York, NY: Harper Reference, 1994.

Fowler, Julianne. *How to Get the Job You Want in Tough Times.* Chicago, IL: Contemporary Books, 1994.

Gieseking, Hal & Paul Plawin. *30 Days to a Good Job.* New York, NY: Simon & Schuster/Fireside, 1994.

Koonce, Richard H. *Career Power: 12 Winning Habits to Get You From Where You Are to Where You Want to Be.* New York: Amacom Books, 1994.

Lowstuter, Clyde C. & David P. Robertson. *Network Your Way to Your Next Job...Fast.* New York, NY: McGraw-Hill Publishing, 1994.

Nadler, Burton Jay. *Naked at the Interview: Tips and Quizzes to Prepare You for Your First Real Job.* New York, NY: John Wiley & Sons, 1994.

Snelling, Robert O., Sr. & Anne M. Snelling. *Jobs! What They Are...Where They Are...What They Pay!* New York, NY: Simon & Schuster/Fireside, 1992.

Spina, Vicki L. *Getting Hired in the '90s: Everything You Always Wanted to Know About Finding a Job But Were Afraid to Ask.* Schaumberg, IL: Corporate Image Publishers, 1994.

Yate, Martin. *Knock 'em Dead — The Ultimate Job Seeker's Handbook.* Holbrook, MA: Bob Adams, Inc. 1994.

————*Beat the Odds.* New York, NY: Ballantine Books, 1994.

APPENDIX 7—SALARY CHART

YEAR	MONTH	WEEK	YEAR	MONTH	WEEK
10000	833.33	192.33	22000	1833.33	423.08
10500	875.00	201.92	22500	1875.00	432.69
11000	916.67	211.54	23000	1916.67	442.31
11500	958.33	221.15	23500	1958.33	451.92
12000	1000.00	230.77	24000	2000.00	461.54
12500	1041.67	240.38	24500	2041.67	471.15
13000	1083.33	250.00	25000	2083.33	480.77
13500	1125.00	259.62	25500	2125.00	490.38
14000	1166.67	269.23	26000	2166.67	500.00
14500	1208.33	278.85	26500	2208.33	509.62
15000	1250.00	288.46	27000	2250.00	519.23
15500	1291.67	298.08	27500	2291.67	528.85
16000	1333.33	307.69	28000	2333.33	538.46
16500	1375.00	317.31	28500	2375.00	548.08
17000	1416.67	326.92	29000	2416.67	557.69
17500	1458.33	336.54	29500	2458.33	567.31
18000	1500.00	346.15	30000	2500.00	576.92
18500	1541.67	355.77	30500	2541.67	586.54
19000	1583.33	365.38	31000	2583.33	596.15
19500	1625.00	375.00	31500	2625.00	605.77
20000	1666.77	384.62	32000	2666.67	615.38
20500	1708.33	394.23	32500	2708.33	625.00
21000	1750.00	403.85	33000	2750.00	634.62
21500	1791.67	413.46	33500	2791.67	644.23

YEAR	MONTH	WEEK	YEAR	MONTH	WEEK
34000	2833.33	653.85	45000	3750.00	865.38
34500	2875.00	663.46	45500	3791.67	875.00
35000	2916.67	673.08	46000	3833.33	884.62
35500	2958.33	682.59	46500	3875.00	894.23
36000	3000.00	692.37	47000	3916.67	903.85
36500	3041.67	701.92	47500	3958.33	913.46
37000	3083.33	711.54	48000	4000.00	923.08
37500	3125.00	721.15	48500	4041.67	932.69
38000	3166.67	730.77	49000	4083.33	942.31
38500	3208.33	740.38	49500	4125.00	951.92
39000	3250.00	750.00	50000	4166.67	961.54
39500	3291.67	759.62	55000	4583.33	1057.69
40000	3333.33	769.23	60000	5000.00	1153.89
40500	3375.00	778.85	65000	5416.66	1250.00
41000	3416.67	788.46	70000	5833.33	1346.15
41500	3458.33	798.08	75000	6250.00	1442.30
42000	3500.00	807.69	80000	6666.66	1538.46
42500	3541.67	817.31	85000	7083.33	1634.61
43000	3583.33	826.92	90000	7500.00	1730.76
43500	3625.00	836.54	95000	7916.66	1826.92
44000	3666.67	846.15	100000	8333.33	1923.07
44500	3708.33	855.57			

BOOKS FOR PROFESSIONAL
CERTIFICATION AND LICENSING

ACCOUNTING

The AICPA's Uniform CPA Exam

REAL ESTATE

Real Estate License Examinations
Math Review for Real Estate License Examinations
Real Estate License SuperCourse

SECURITIES

Registered Representative / Stockbroker

TEACHING

CBEST: California Basic Educational Skills Test
NTE / Praxis II
PPST / Praxis I
Teacher Certification Tests

OTHER PROFESSIONS

Automobile Technician Certification Tests
Counselor
Refrigeration License Examinations
Truck Driver's Guide to Commercial Driver Licensing

AVAILABLE AT BOOKSTORES EVERYWHERE

MACMILLAN • USA

OFFICE GUIDES

Office Guide to
Business English

Office Guide to
Business Letters, Memos & Reports

Office Guide to
Business Math

Office Guide to
Spelling & Word Division

AVAILABLE AT BOOKSTORES EVERYWHERE

MACMILLAN • USA

BOOKS FOR GRADUATE SCHOOL AND BEYOND

ARCO's SuperCourses

GMAT SuperCourse
GRE SuperCourse
LSAT SuperCourse
MCAT SuperCourse
TOEFL SuperCourse

ARCO's Cram Courses

GMAT Cram Course
GRE Cram Course
LSAT Cram Course

TOEFL

TOEFL: Test of English as a Foreign Language
TOEFL Grammar Workbook
TOEFL Reading and Vocabulary Workbook
TOEFL Skills for Top Scores

Teacher Certification

CBEST: California Educational Basic Skills Test
NTE / Praxis II
PPST / Praxis I
Teacher Certification Tests

Health Professions

Allied Health Professions
Nursing School Entrance Examinations
PCAT: Pharmacy College Admission Test

Graduate School Guides

The Best Graduate Business Schools
The Best Law Schools
Getting into Law School Today
Getting into Medical School
The Transfer Student's Guide to Changing Colleges

Graduate & Professional School Entrance

GMAT: Graduate Management Admission Test
GRE: Graduate Record Examination
GRE • GMAT Math Review
Graduate Record Examination in Psychology
GRE • LSAT Logic Workbook
LSAT: Law School Admission Test
MAT: Miller Analogies Test
MCAT Sample Exams

AVAILABLE AT BOOKSTORES EVERYWHERE

MACMILLAN • USA

CIVIL SERVICE BOOKS

TEST PREPARATION

Accountant / Auditor
ACWA: Administrative Careers With America
Air Traffic Controller
American Foreign Service Officer
Beginning Clerical Worker
Bookkeeper / Account Clerk
Building Custodian / Building Superintendent /
   Custodian Engineer
Bus Operator / Conductor
Case Worker
Correction Officer
Correction Officer Promotion Tests
Court Officer / Senior Court Officer /
   Court Clerk
Electrician / Electrician's Helper
Emergency Dispatcher / 911 Operator
File Clerk / General Clerk
Fire Department Lieutenant / Captain /
   Battalion Chief
Firefighter
Law Enforcement Exams Handbook
Mail Handler / Mail Processor
Maintenance Worker / Mechanical Maintainer
Police Officer
Police Sergeant / Lieutenant / Captain
Postal Clerk and Carrier
Postal Exams Handbook

Principal Administrative Associate /
   Administrative Assistant
Probation Officer / Parole Officer
Railroad Clerk
Railroad Porter/ Cleaner
Sanitation Worker
Special Agent / Treasury Enforcement Agent
State Trooper / Highway Patrol Officer /
   State Traffic Officer
Storekeeper / Stock Handler
Track Worker
Traffic Enforcement Agent

CAREERS / STUDY GUIDES

Civil Service Administrative Tests
Civil Service Arithmetic and Vocabulary
Civil Service Handbook
Civil Service Tests for Basic Skills Jobs
Clerical Exams Handbook
Federal Civil Service Jobs: The Complete
   Guide
Federal Jobs for College Graduates
Federal Jobs in Law Enforcement
General Test Practice for 101 U.S. Jobs
Practice for Clerical, Typing, and
   Stenographic Tests
Writing Your SF 171: The Federal
   Employment Application Form

AVAILABLE AT BOOKSTORES EVERYWHERE

MACMILLAN • USA